Re-creating Christmas
A DIY Outreach for Churches of Any Size

Tammy Tilley

Warner Press, Inc.
Anderson, Indiana

Warner Press, Inc.
Warner Press and "Warner Press" logo are trademarks of Warner Press, Inc.

Re-creating Christmas
A DIY Outreach for Churches of Any Size

Requests for information should be sent to:
Warner Press, Inc.
2902 Enterprise Dr.
P.O. Box 2499
Anderson, IN 46013
www.warnerpress.org

Cover and Layout Designer: Curtis Corzine
Editors: Tammy Tilley, Robin Fogle

ISBN: 978-1-68434-173-3
Printed in USA

warner press®

MADE IN THE USA

Contents

Acknowledgments

We at Warner Press are grateful and appreciative of the churches who have not hesitated to share their resources with us in the creation of this book. Namely, Southeast Church in Louisville: You provided a Christmas outreach for years, and when it had run its course, you were gracious enough simply to hand over your information to Eastside Church of God, Anderson, Indiana. If any of these materials look familiar, that's because some of it originated with you. Thank you for doing the hard work by bringing ideas to life and then passing them on.

Eastside Church of God and Mary Ann Randolph: You paid it forward by sharing not only a portion of the text, but also verbal ideas and words of encouragement. You even allowed video cameras to invade your outreach for a few hours so we could get footage of your own Christmas outreach. We're sure cameras weren't around in AD 1! After several years of creating your own outreach and fine-tuning your efforts, you make it look easy. Never have you wavered from your original intentions of offering an experiential opportunity for families to witness what Bethlehem and Jesus' entrance into our reality looked and felt like. Even more, you are gospel-focused, with your hearts desiring we come to know Jesus as Savior. May God bless all you do, and when we celebrate in Heaven, may your line of grateful people be very long as the redeemed thank you for sharing the Good News.

For the other churches who took some time to share stories and wisdom from your own outreach experiences: Discovery Baptist Church in Gig Harbor, Washington; GraceWay Bible Church in Hamilton, New Jersey; Maple Grove Church of God in Anderson, Indiana; Searcy First Assembly in Searcy, Arkansas; and Mountain Park Church in Phoenix, Arizona: We're grateful God's family extends well beyond geographical lines and church walls. Together, we love God and do all we can to love His children. Thank you.

It's always been about Jesus, and it always will be. So many have made this effort a priority because we see the potential Kingdom impact. From product development to marketing, sales, and everyone in between who crunch numbers or get the product ready to be sent out, thank you. May the Kingdom grow because of your dedication to putting resources into the hands of our churches.

In Christ Alone,
Your Warner Press Family

Introduction

This book places in your hand the opportunity to dream, pray, and create a Christmas outreach for neighbors and an entire community no matter the size of your church or budget. We provide the thinking, outline, ideas, online assistance, and encouragement. All you need are some volunteers, a little bit of money, and a DIY attitude. There's no need to purchase an expensive kit when you invest in this one book.

Whether your church attendance barely reaches 80 people, or your Sunday attendance is well over 800 or more, use this book to help guide you through the details so you can create a new and exciting way for your community to experience the meaning and relevance of that first Christmas.

But why bother? Why go through the effort?

As a Christ-follower, you understand the significance of Christmas: Had there been no Christmas, there would have been no Easter. Had there been neither, we would not have a way back to the Savior. Since you understand the importance of the story as so much bigger than a cute little Baby being born in a stable with curious onlookers gathered around, you want to share the story and its meaning with the world.

This is the most important story, after all. Jesus left Heaven's perfection and communion with His Father to enter the world as a Baby. Only a mysterious, bright star gave a clue to the whereabouts of His location. Only a few ragamuffin shepherd boys were visited by a heavenly host announcing this earth-shattering birth. Mary and Joseph? They had little forewarning themselves, each visited by an angel who offered a message that their lives were about to change.

This story unfolded, creating the very first Christmas. And we continue to talk about it today, over 2,000 years later. Whether or not the world dares to admit it, Christmas is rooted in the reality of a Savior, of God Himself taking on flesh and entering our world so someday we could enter His.

This is fabulous news, we well know. Still, each year we see decorations line department store shelves before the leaves have turned colors in the fall; we read blogs about the hottest toys on the market, the trendiest clothes to buy, and the glorious gadgets everyone "must have" all in the name of Christmas. And at the end of the season as others pack away the decorations and study the financial cost of the holiday, we cannot help but wonder where it all went wrong. We think, "If they only knew the real peace, joy, and hope Christmas can bring.... If my neighbor only knew the answer to their problems and pain.... If only...."

Then there's all the technology that makes life seem glamorous with everybody connected and entertained. The world operates on techno-time. We play games on our gaming consoles. We perform work obligations on our computers. We keep the family schedule, recipes, and budgets on our tablets, stay in touch on our watches and watch television on our phones. Somewhere along the way, we wonder how in the world the church can compete with all the noise in our culture.

Speaking of culture, we need only look up the street to the neighbor's house to get just a small glimpse of our unraveling world. With fighting families, social anxieties, financial stress, and yes, addiction, competition, and physical illness, we want to help. We want to offer answers. We really want to point them to THE answer.

We doubt the seeking would accept an invitation to church. Statistics show a steep decline in church attendance. Many find the church irrelevant or unhelpful. Of those newcomers who do give us a try, more often than not they arrive because their children showed up first, through a friend or because a neighbor extended an invitation.

Even more, our schools are feeling the pressure more and more to remove any and every reflection of the Christian Christmas story from plays and musicals. One example involves a Northern Indiana high school where the music department included a nativity scene in its program for 30 years. A few years ago, a parent, on behalf of his child, sued the school. After a long battle and even an appeal, the courts ruled the school could no longer continue its long-held tradition.

So how do we redeem the Christmas season? How do we point our neighbors, school communities, and family members back to Jesus in any sort of resonant, meaningful way?

This book provides part of the answer: We plop them right in the middle of the Christmas story. We set the scene, costume the characters, and enable them to EXPERIENCE the story. They become part of the narrative of Jesus coming to earth for them. Nothing is quite as personal or powerful.

And it's fun! By offering this experience, Scripture comes to life. Unbelievers, skeptics, and seekers bring their kids, and as a family, they hear the angel shout, "Fear not!" They smell the baking bread or the stinky stable. They come against the mighty Roman soldiers and more, until they arrive at the place where the Baby Jesus rests.

As mentioned above, this book provides only part of the answer. The other part of the answer comes from you. Enthusiasm is contagious, so once your church has committed, start talking it up, both within the congregation and within the community. Determine not to allow Satan to overwhelm or create discouragement. He will try, but as a strong, Christ-focused body, rebuke any evil power that tries to destroy what is already rightfully God's.

Pray over the process. Ask God to bless it, and He will. Let's take back Christmas for the Kingdom's sake. Let's give people an eternal reason to celebrate.

Let's re-create the real Christmas.

Added Note:

When you purchase this book, you have access to numerous online items to help you with your event.

These resources include:

- Organizational spreadsheet
- Promotional video for your church
- Invitations in three sizes
- Poster
- Newspaper Ad
- Door Hanger
- Web Banner
- Church Banner
- Construction Tutorials
- Costume Tutorials
- Recipes
- Printable Activity Sheets

…and more! Visit WarnerPress.org/RecreatingChristmas-freeresources.

Chapter 1

Background Information on Bethlehem in AD 1

Our church has added a few different things throughout the years. One year we added a bounce house and giant inflatable slide themed around winter. But always at the forefront of our minds is to present the Christmas story as authentically as possible. We really do try to re-create Bethlehem as it might have been when Jesus was born. When visitors experience what the first Christmas was really like, the story of the Baby born in a manger becomes real to them.

—Mary Ann Randolph, Pastor of Church Life and Discipleship,
Eastside Church of God, Anderson, IN

Understanding the sights and sounds of Bethlehem when Christ was born obviously offers an ideal backdrop for your church's efforts in re-creating the scenes. While visitors may have to imagine some characteristics, your knowledge of this town where the Savior came into the world will help them realize Jesus arrived at the perfect time and in God's perfect plan:

> *But when the set time had fully come, God sent his Son, born of a woman, born under the law, to redeem those under the law, that we might receive adoption to sonship.*
> —Galatians 4:4–5

> *The time has come.... The kingdom of God has come near.* —Mark 1:15

The Town of Bethlehem

The name "Bethlehem" means "House of Bread" or "Bread House." The Bible not only reflects bread as a staple in the Jewish diet, but more importantly, Jesus is often referred to as "The Bread of Life."

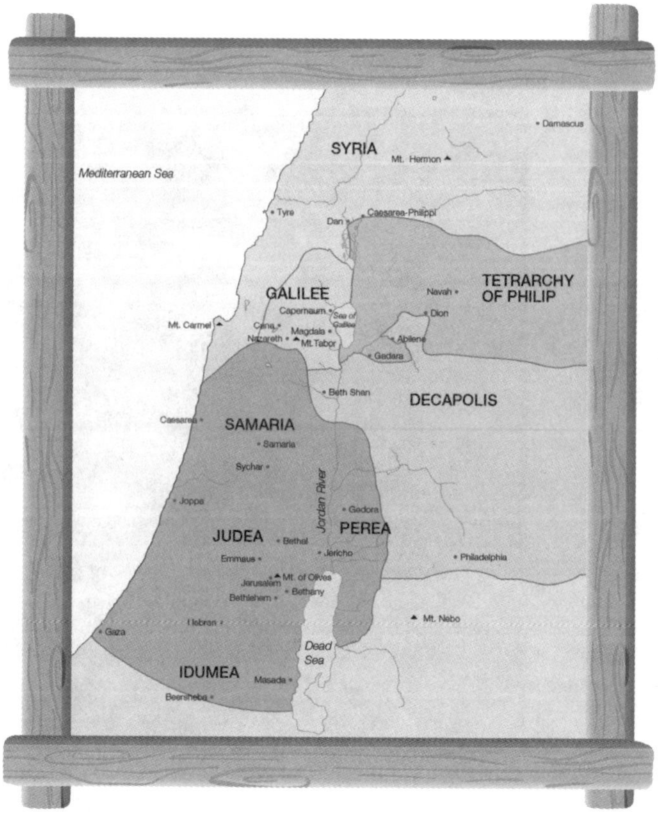

The town of Bethlehem is located five miles southwest of Jerusalem, on the main highway to Hebron and Egypt. When Jesus arrived, the population was only between 300 and 1,000 citizens, so Bethlehem truly was a little town.

Bethlehem is also situated 2,550 feet above sea level in the hill country of Judea. The hill-sides are naturally terraced and dotted with caves. The soil is very fertile and productive, the hillsides filled with fig trees, vines, and olive and almond groves.

The climate of the area varied. The expansive territory where the Israelites made their home was filled with hill country where the winters were bitterly cold; coastal plains, where the morning dews watered the fields; and a river valley, where the climate was tropical. Summers were primarily hot and dry, while winters were cold and wet.

Housing

People lived and often worked from their homes. Houses typically were one room, but second stories were not uncommon; ladders or stairways led to the second floor or roof, referenced in the Bible as an "upper room."

Homes were built to meet the demands of climate and the limitations of money and materials. Much of the year was very hot and dry; therefore, homes were built to keep out the heat.

Floors were made from brushed earth, clay, packed mud, or plaster. One or two narrow windows sat within the structure to allow the breeze to pass through and were shuttered to keep out the sun. Windows also functioned as chimneys in some homes.

Doors were narrow and short, made of wood, hinged on stone sockets. Thresholds were made of stone. A mezuzah (a metal or wooden box) was affixed to the door post, locked with a large wooden key, and secured by a wooden bar behind the door. Doing so fulfilled the Scripture from Deuteronomy 6:9 that reads, *Write [God's commandments] on the doorframes of your houses and on your gates.*

The mud roofs were flat with rails around the edges (such as lattice). Sometimes they were used as a family room and also for drying laundry, sleeping during hot weather, drying raisins, figs, and flax, and for saying prayers.

Walls were made from dried mud or clay bricks, either rectangular or square. Inside, the walls were very stark, containing wooden or stone shelves, or built-in cubby holes.

Yards were commonly small and decorated with shrubs, flowers, or trees. Some yards held gardens to grow food.

Furnishings were few. Maybe a chest was situated in a corner to hold a variety of provisions. The dinner table consisted of a straw mat or animal skin; beds were also made from straw or animal skin but were rolled up during the day and stored against the wall. Blankets were made from goat skin folded over and stuffed with wool or feathers.

Cooking utensils usually consisted of different sizes of earthen jars with wide and narrow mouths used for cooking and storage. Olive oil was stored in a specially designed vessel. Bowls were made of wood or clay, knives and forks of metal and wood.

Other items the Israelites might have had in their homes include a type of hand mill for grinding grain or a large stone mortar and pestle that was kept on the floor.

Lamps, providing dim light at best, were typically made from clay and held both olive oil and a linen wick for burning, giving a sweet aroma throughout the house. If a family could afford it, the lamp might be placed on a tall stand or upon a wooden or stone shelf on the wall.

Taxes
Jews were weighed down by having to deal with many taxes. Their first obligation was to God, but Rome demanded their due as well. In New Testament times, Rome levied taxes on the entire known world in order to maintain its vast army, building projects, and emperor. Tax collectors who worked for the Romans were distrusted and despised, for they cheated taxpayers into paying more money than they owed. The second tax to which Jews were subjected was the Temple tax, and it applied to every male over the age of twelve.

Although the Jews were overtaxed, they never complained about their tithes to God and the Temple tax. Unfortunately for them, taxes did not stop there. Their tax money paid for roads, waterways, bridges, and also for whatever Caesar wanted. Caesar implemented a road tax, property tax, water tax, city tax, and even a death tax! There were also taxes on imports and exports on any items from the market place.

Census
Caesar ordered for a census to be taken every 14 years. Rome wanted to keep careful tabs on all of its citizens. A census kept track of births and deaths; Caesar Augustus wouldn't want to miss out on any taxes! The census took Joseph and Mary to Bethlehem from the town of Nazareth in Galilee, about 70 miles. Because Joseph was Jewish, he had to register in the town from where his ancestors came. Bethlehem was the town of David, and Joseph belonged to David's lineage.

Shopping
Shopping in Bethlehem was similar to our visiting farmers' markets today. People sold their specialty items from their shops just outside their homes.

Bargaining and trading items was very common. Although there were several forms of currency, trading was widely practiced. People might trade fish for some bread, jewelry for candy, or clothes for food.

Transportation
The most popular mode of transportation in ancient times was simply walking! Most people could not afford an animal, so when they needed to make a trip, they put on their sandals. All this walking made for some pretty dirty feet, which is why it was customary to have feet washed when entering a home.

The People of Bethlehem

Greetings

Communication was very important for people in the Bible. When two people met on the road, it was not polite to nod and pass. This behavior would have been an insult to the other person. Instead, they would say "hello" and "goodbye" and try to be as polite as possible. Conversations and meetings could have taken hours.

"SHALOM" (generally meaning "peace") was a face to face greeting, possibly with a hand gesture, but without physical contact.

A formal kiss or a double cheek kiss was exchanged between males.

Bowing was done to individuals as a matter of courtesy. The bow would be done with a slight bend of the waist, not on their knees. People would normally bow to someone who was very respected, like a rabbi.

Size and Strength

Compared to Americans, Israelites in the Bible times were small in stature. Although they were smaller and thinner, they were not weak.

Since power tools didn't exist, everything was done by hand. Everyone worked hard, including the girls. Every day, young women filled their water jugs at the local well and carried them home on their heads. When filled with water, each jug weighed as much as fifty pounds! Another strenuous activity was preparing grain for food. An ideal wife of that day was one with strong arms (Proverbs 31:17).

The Family

The family was composed of all who claimed kinship with the father of a household: the wife, children, his unmarried brothers and sisters, parents, other relatives, and servants. The family was the central unit of Hebrew society.

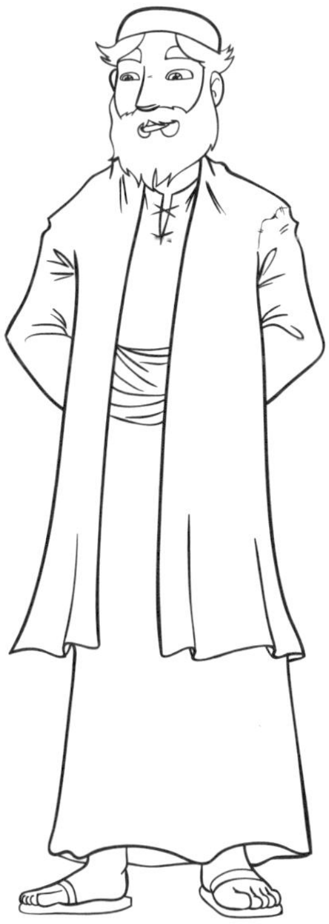

Because of the census, some distant members of the family may have been in town, and houses would have been even more crowded than normal.

Men

A man's day, for the most part, was wrapped up in the job he held. In a land where famines were common, the change of seasons and the weather patterns were noticed carefully. Many men would plan their lives around the season they were in. To lead his family, a man would pay close attention to the calendar for feasts and holy days.

Fathers were responsible for teaching their sons a trade from the time they were born. It was said that if a man did not teach his son a useful trade, he was raising the boy to become a thief. If a father had many sons and one was interested in a different trade, the father would apprentice the boy to another man to learn his trade.

A father was both a possessor and master. His will was binding upon the community that was the family. A man's strength and authority were carried on in his sons. Therefore, there was an emphasis on bearing many children.

Women

A woman's work truly was never done. Every day she would be busy in the home taking care of her family. Children needed to be taken care of and food needed to be prepared for the whole family. The women were also responsible for many of the errands (trips to the market and the well) that needed to be carried out. Many hours were spent in household chores. Half of her day might be spent making bread and maintaining her family's home.

A mother's primary duty was to bear children. She also possessed considerable authority over the family and was due the respect and honor of her husband and children. She named the children and was responsible for their early education. She was exempt from Sabbath labor. If there were no male heirs, the woman could inherit and become a landowner in her own right.

Children

Children worked around the home doing the everyday chores. They used goat-skin buckets and went to the well early in the day to draw water before it became too hot. Children also sorted corn seeds from the poisonous "tars" that were mixed in with the grain. They played various types of games in the streets. They could play with balls, whistles, rattles, wheels, and dolls.

Daughters learned homemaking skills such as baking, spinning, and weaving, from their mother. Making butter, cheese, drying fruit, saving garden seeds, and packing fish were just a few things a girl needed to be able to do in order to manage her own house.

Tax Collectors

The job of the tax collector was a goal for ambitious men, but with it came ridicule. A tax collector would calculate and gather taxes for Rome. They were notorious for overcharging people and keeping any extra funds. As a result, these men were both hated and feared.

Rabbis

"Rabbi" was a title given to Jewish teachers. They knew the Scriptures well, especially passages of the Law, and they were eager to pray for anyone who needed it. The title was a way to honor them for the position they had achieved. They walked through the market place often to meet and greet the people, and in return, they were usually greeted with a bow of respect from others.

Social Life and Customs

Birth

Childlessness was always regarded as a calamity, and it was considered that one's happiness was proportionate to the number of children, particularly sons. A daughter was not so welcome because of her subordinate position. She was an asset to the family only as a worker. At birth, salt was rubbed into the baby's skin to make it firm, and it was closely wrapped in "swaddling cloths" to make its limbs grow straight. The child received a carefully chosen name which indicated some presumed moral or physical property. After eight days, a boy was circumcised. Children were not weaned until age two or three.

Marriage

Marriages were arranged by the parents, and social mixing between the genders was uncommon. It was the duty of everyone to marry. Because the bride was a working asset, she had to be paid for. First was the formal and binding ceremony of betrothal with an exchange of gifts. When the wedding day came, the bridegroom and his friends went in procession to the bride's home, where she and her family were waiting. The couple was blessed, and the bridegroom led the bride through the village to his own home with the invited guests lining the way to make a torchlight procession. A great feast followed, which might last as long as a week.

Death

A death in the household set in motion an elaborate ceremony of mourning. Professional mourners might be hired to weep and wail. The body was washed and clothed, sometimes anointed, and wrapped in special grave clothes with a linen napkin bound around the head. The body was buried within 24 hours. The poor were buried in common graves or in caves. The wealthy had tombs specially hewn out of rock and sealed with a boulder.

Old Age

The Hebrews held their elders in honor. They were respected for their wisdom and experience. This honor was not simply because of the outward sign of gray hair, but also because of the attainment of "fullness of days," which was considered to be a sign of divine favor for fearing the Lord and keeping His commands. Older men were expected to lead in positions of authority and responsibility as elders.

Meals and Food

Generally, two meals were served daily, although a third was not uncommon. The first meal of the day could be served at any time from early morning until noon. It came after the work of the morning was completed or when the noonday heat made work too difficult. The evening meal was served when the day's work ended. This was usually the principal meal of the Hebrews.

Chapter 7 discusses specific foods eaten during the time when Jesus was born. God had abundantly blessed His children with wonderful, healthy food to enjoy!

The Currency in Bethlehem

Many forms of currency were used in Bethlehem. Jewish, Greek, and Roman currency were all in circulation. Many times, someone with one type of currency was unable to spend it until they had it converted by the money changer. This is still seen in modern times. For example, those living in northern states like Michigan often receive Canadian coins. Since these coins can't be used in vending machines, it is necessary to trade them in for U.S. currency. This was true but on a larger scale in Bethlehem.

While Bethlehem had coins of different value, the most common coin was a denarius, a Roman silver coin worth a day's wage. When shopkeepers in Re-creating Christmas discuss the prices of their wares, if they choose, they can discuss in terms of denarii. They can speak to the cost of their goods and the sacrifice neighboring customers make in purchasing the goods in the marketplace. Some churches create "play" denarii and offer a handful of change to guests to use for purchasing items once they enter Bethlehem.

> *My family attended church when I was a child, so I grew up hearing the Christmas story. When I had my own family, we went to a live event, and it was like I was awakened from a slumber. It was like I was hearing it for the first time. Now my kids are grown, but we continue to go each Christmas. I still get goosebumps, and I still cry whenever I see the little Baby with live animals all around.*
>
> —Melissa, Attendee

Chapter 2

Casting the Vision: The Overview

We started very small our first year, with just our youth group. Bethlehem consisted of a few kids and a couple of dolls. Twenty-five people came, and we thought we were a great success. The next year, we thought we'd have a choir!... It rained, and they sang in the rain wearing white sheets, soaked and dripping. The following year, we added plywood store-fronts, and God orchestrated something on a crazy level. I'm still stunned. We're a church of 200 people including kids and the elderly. Over 5,000 people come to our event.

—Gayle Shriner, Discovery Baptist, Gig Harbor, WA

Whether your church sits on Main Street in a town of 3,000, downtown in a large metropolitan area, or beside a country cornfield, you are about to embark on an incredible journey. Who wouldn't be excited to share the greatest news of all time, the answer to every question, the solution to every problem?

> *Grace was given us in Christ Jesus before the beginning of time, but it has now been revealed through the appearing of our Savior, Christ Jesus, who has destroyed death and has brought life and immortality to light through the gospel.* —2 Timothy 1:9–10

We know the reality of our Savior's redeeming grace, and we have the privilege of telling others about Him. The problem is, many people today choose not to go to church; however, they just might enjoy a community event. They might see God as distant and uncaring, and we can show them His love. They might even believe the story of Jesus coming to earth as mythical, and we can point them to His reality.

Bringing the Christmas story to life and guiding others to see themselves in the story—in God's story—aids seekers in considering that this Jesus thing just might be true, and if it's true, they begin to see Jesus as real and approachable. One of the things Jesus does in Scripture is hang out with those seeking to find wholeness and fulfillment in their lives. The same is true today as we become like Jesus, showing others His love. The more we love, the more we interact, the more lost people are drawn to Him.

This is why we endeavor to offer this outreach to our neighbors and friends.

The Leaders

Of course, you might understand the important reasons for an outreach such as Re-creating Christmas, but other churchgoers may not see the vision on their own. Communicating the "why" is important for the church body to understand the effort behind the outreach. Bottom line: While people in our community might know the Christmas story, these days it seems the story doesn't quite hold the impact to change their lives if it's told in the same way it's always been told. If the church is willing to present the same story in a new way, that effort will capture people's attention and potentially help turn their hearts toward the Savior.

One of the best ways to generate interest in Re-creating Christmas is to show the pastoral team the free promotional video found online at WarnerPress.org/RecreatingChristmas-fre-eresources. This video is designed specifically for people inside the church walls in order to communicate the significance of the event as well as cultivate a desire for the congregation to be involved. Begin with the pastoral team, and once they're on board, with their guidance, the video can be shown to the church body.

Of course, the most important person leading the charge for Re-creating Christmas is the lead pastor. If he is excited, the congregation will get excited. The more he talks about the outreach, especially from the pulpit on a Sunday morning, the more energy will be generated, and more people will get involved. Make sure not just the lead pastor, but all the church staff, catch the vision and understand the significance of the event so they too can share it with others.

After the senior staff get behind the event, there needs to be a team of people who can make the outreach happen. They don't carry all the weight, but they are the faces the rest of the church come to know as event coordinators and can come to them with questions, suggestions, or express interest in involvement. And while the structure is necessary so chaos doesn't prevail, people get excited when they are involved, so include as many people as possible in supporting roles.

Most of us have been in leadership positions enough to know not everyone can lead, but we do need an individual, a visionary, a point person who can see the big picture. This person may or may not be involved in every detail, which is why this individual, called the event director, organizes a team. It's also important the event director reminds everyone along the way that the goal for the outreach is to bring the story of Jesus' birth to lost people. Everyone wants to celebrate Christmas; giving them the real reason for celebrating Christmas is the purpose for Re-creating Christmas. This person might be appropriate for taking care of the budget as well, but he or she might choose a money-wise person for taking care of the budget.

The event director then appoints several other key people, namely, someone who can oversee the details of the event, or the administrator, and someone who can coordinate publicity and hospitality. If your church is small, the event director might take on other primary tasks as well, either as the administrator, or hospitality and publicity. If this is the case, the event director should do his/her best to keep the event a manageable size.

From this beginning team—the lead pastor and staff; the event director; and two or three assistants—other committees can be established. The flow chart below can help in outlining the structure:

Re-creating Christmas Flow Chart

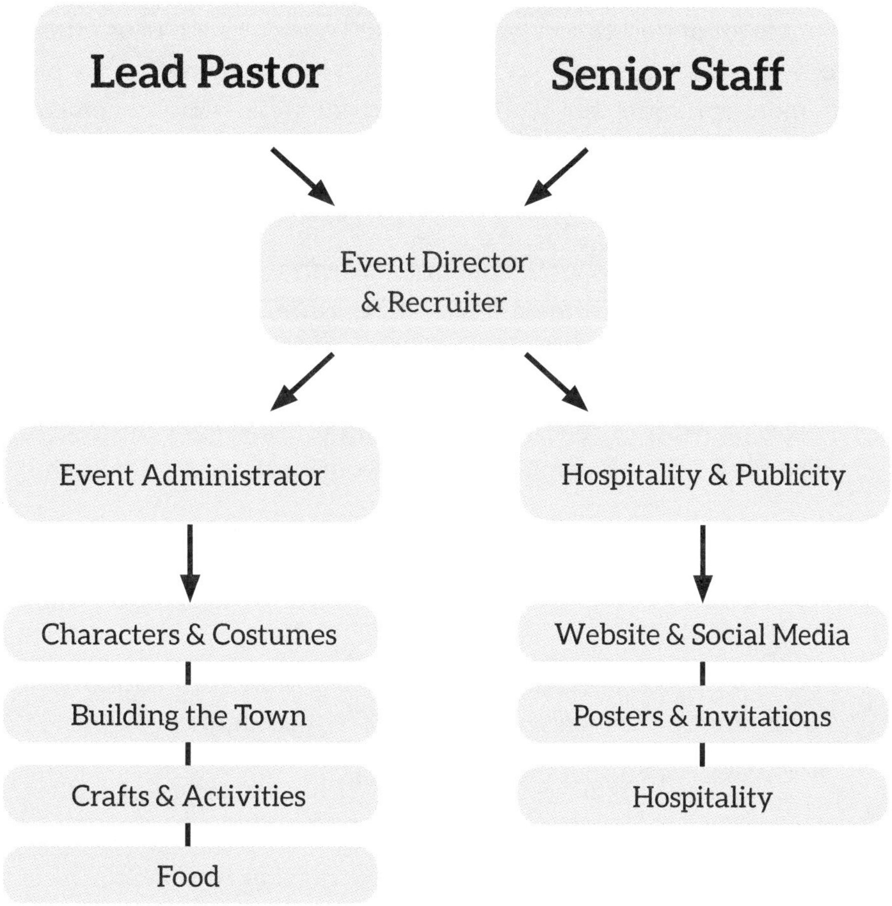

This chart shows the basic structure of your outreach. A more complete view is on page 28.

When to Schedule Your Outreach

Scheduling your outreach depends primarily on the best days your community will attend, particularly the unchurched. Smaller communities won't want to schedule on the same day as a school event that most families are connected to. Suburban and urban areas might want to consider not scheduling on the weekend after Thanksgiving, as many people like to shop on Black Friday.

Typically, families with young children will attend an event earlier in the day or evening so as not to interfere with bedtime. Older audiences usually prefer the later times.

If you're holding the event for more than one day, the weekend is probably the best time to offer the outreach. Consider a Friday and Saturday and invite your guests back to church on Sunday.

More ambitious volunteers might want to offer the event on Christmas Eve in place of a Christmas Eve service. Still others might enjoy hosting the event on a Sunday prior to Christmas.

Strategies for getting the word out are discussed in chapter 11.

The Timeline

Depending on your level of dedication, you can plan your outreach in as little as four months, but in order to be successful, you will need to be dedicated to the process. Longer than four months is ideal, but when God ordains steps, time becomes less relevant and obedience becomes paramount!

One way to organize the details is to create a spreadsheet. Create a timeline and include as many details as possible. A free, downloadable organizational spreadsheet is available at WarnerPress.org/RecreatingChristmas-freeresources. You can adjust the spreadsheet for your own specifications.

The timeline below is based on a four-month planning window. Obviously, you want to adjust your timeline based on the complexity of the outreach, such as how the town will be built.

4 Months out:

- Pray!
- Set a goal for the number of people you want to try to reach and the communities where you will take the message.
- Establish a budget (see Chapter 3).
- Make a list of needs and a list of volunteers.
- Decide on location, either inside or outside the church.
- Show the promotional video to your congregation (found online at WarnerPress.org/RecreatingChristmas-freeresources). Begin encouraging churchgoers to sign up immediately; provide the list of volunteers and skills needed. Don't be afraid to make phone calls and tap specific people on the shoulder.

3 Months out:

- Keep praying!
- Begin making the scenes.
- Decide on how to source costumes.
- Ask your church to begin inviting people by word of mouth.
- Create a Facebook page, Instagram, and/or a website. Make the name as simple as Recreating Christmas in (your town's name). Post something every day.

2 Months out:

- Immerse your event in prayer.
- Provide churchgoers with invitations to hand out everywhere they go. Download free artwork for the invitation at WarnerPress.org/RecreatingChristmas-freeresources.

- Hang posters everywhere allowable—in grocery stores, offices, schools, restaurants, coffee houses, bars, and even other churches. Download free artwork for the poster at WarnerPress.org/RecreatingChristmas-freeresources.
- Purchase ad space in the local newspaper. Download free artwork for the newspaper ad at WarnerPress.org/RecreatingChristmas-freeresources.
- Continue posting on Facebook, Instagram, and website.
- Continue working on volunteers, scenes, and costumes.
- Hand out specific instructions and/or scripts that have not yet been provided.
- Create a follow-up plan for guests (involve church staff).

1 Month out:

- Pray again!
- Reach out to volunteers. What do they need? What are their questions?
- Continue encouraging others to reach out into the community. Generate energy!
- Ask the lead pastor for input regarding a post-event follow-up plan.

1 Week out:

- Put up the scenes and prepare other areas, such as the entryway or kitchen.
- Have a dress rehearsal.
- Don't forget to pray!

The Day of:

- Embrace the day, finalize any last-minute issues, and in faith, believe Jesus is going to change lives!
- Remind volunteers to stay positive.
- Remind actors to stay in-character.
- Exude joy!
- Welcome guests and practice hospitality.
- Implement the follow-up plan.

Let the event stand for itself. Just offer the experience and let visitors step into its reality. As individuals leave, offer an invitation for the Sunday service where they will sing Christmas songs and hear the gospel message.

A Different Approach:

One out-of-the-box idea in establishing a Re-creating Christmas outreach is to partner with another local church. This idea is especially good if your church has a small congregation.

In doing so, denominational walls come crumbling down and the siloed "us" and "them" mentality disappears. Two church groups collaborating together on a single project send the message that you stand unified within your community for reaching others for Christ. Who's right and who's wrong on doctrinal positions become secondary to the greatest commandment Jesus lays out for us.

When churches co-labor, they grow in understanding and friendship with one another. In regard to the outreach itself, they double up resources, finances, and leadership. They realize they can do more together in this context than a single church can do on its own. Most of all, Christians multiply their prayer efforts. When we pray, God unleashes His saving power on the Earth, His children grow in His likeness, and unbelieving hearts come to believe in the saving grace of Christ.

While we might see the validity of all these claims and even believe them, we still need structure as we join efforts. Obviously, someone has to take the lead, initiate the process, and then delegate. Consider this possible scenario:

1. Your senior pastor and leader of the event invite the pastor of the other church to a meeting to discuss the outreach possibility.
2. Upon meeting, present the concept and the possibility of partnering together. Be clear and concise in your vision and goals.
3. Discuss the specifics as to how you want to partner. Consider leading with a sentence similar to: "This is what we are asking for from you" or "Here are ways we hope you will partner with us."
4. Listen with humility and be willing to negotiate on a few areas.
5. Cover with prayer.

Talk about making an impression on the community! One of the most loving things a congregation can do is extend the hand of fellowship to a neighboring church and at the same time send the message to unbelievers that we co-labor for God's Kingdom. When unbelievers see Christ-followers from different congregations come together in love and service, they see the gospel being lived out, and they cannot help but be curious.

Curiosity just might grow into conviction, which cultivates confession, which then leads to redemption.

> *Give his people the knowledge of salvation through the forgiveness of their sins, because of the tender mercy of our God…to shine on those living in darkness and in the shadow of death, to guide our feet into the path of peace.* —Luke 1:77–79

> *I started going to church because of [the Re-creating Christmas event]. I found an amazing group of people inside the church. I was raising four kids on my own. Now I'm a Christian and my kids have this whole extended family of grandparents, aunts and uncles, and cousins from my church. This all happened because I made the choice to go to their Christmas event.*
>
> —Name Withheld

Nativity Christmas Tree

Decorate with different types of nativity sets

Chapter 3

Establishing a Budget: The Dollars & Sense

> *Now that we've been doing [our Christmas outreach] for a while, people in our church give weekly during the offering or online to this project throughout the year.... It's pretty amazing how people will donate their time to help build scenes or make costumes.*
>
> —Fran Emmons, GraceWay Bible Church, Hamilton, NJ

Believe it or not, finances are not the deal-breaker for your Christmas outreach. Sure, it would be fabulous if your church budget held a line item for the occasion; money is necessary to pull off a community-wide event. However, the first question shouldn't be, "How are we going to pay for it?" On the other hand, neither should the assumption be, "We'll just do it and worry about the money later." May the Giver of all good things provide us with wisdom as we think about what it means to be good stewards of what He has freely and graciously provided.

> *You shall tithe all the yield of your seed that comes from the field year by year. And before the LORD your God, in the place that he will choose, to make his name dwell there, you shall eat the tithe of your grain, of your wine, and of your oil, and the firstborn of your herd and flock, that you may learn to fear the LORD your God always.* —Deuteronomy 14:22–23 (ESV)

With some entrepreneurial effort, people using their natural gifts and skills, and a spirit of stewardship, your church can embark on Re-creating Christmas and not break the bank. As a matter of fact, most of the churches interviewed began with sparse funding, and as the energy grew, so did the financial commitment. Of the few churches who started with a larger budget, they chose to spend money in ways other churches would not necessarily have to spend.

Gayle Shriner, a volunteer from Discovery Baptist Church in Gig Harbor, Washington, relates, "We had zero budget our first year, so we thrived on whatever people would donate." Later, the church would establish a line in their budget, as deacon David Christensen attests: "We made all our costumes, used tents for buildings, and built structures. Props either were purchased or donated over the years as we grew in presentation. We budget $2,000 per year for this event and hold to that fairly close. All cast and labor for set up and cleanup is donated time."

Fran Emmons from GraceWay Bible Church in Hamilton, New Jersey, said the 350-member church she attends prioritized a quality sound system because they held a gathering at different places throughout the evening: "I looked at everything we needed and wrote it down.... Initially, our budget was pretty steep because we rented a sound system. Our church eventually purchased its own sound system, so that helped our bottom line tremendously."

Many churches will not need to prioritize a sound system as GraceWay chose to do; nevertheless, organizers of the outreach will need to think about resourcing several aspects of the event. The remainder of this chapter outlines those areas and offers creative ways of saving money.

Costumes

- Visit thrift stores, especially on half-price days, for decorations, sheets, towels, and fabric for costumes, and if you're fortunate, even tents and tables.
- Ask the local school's family science department or 4-H club to help sew the costumes.
- Order fabric by the bolt through a local fabric store who has the flexibility to sell it at wholesale price. Some local stores might even be willing to donate the fabric or offer it at cost.

Structures

- Ask local businesses to donate their pallets, as they usually dispose of these wooden items. You can tear them apart to build storefronts, homes, and the nativity stable.
- Look through online garage sale sites for individuals who want to sell lumber, canopies, or tents. They might be willing to negotiate their price if they know the reason their goods are being used.
- Ask churchgoers to borrow or donate tents and canopies.
- Ask the local Boy Scouts to donate their time and help secure the structures.

Decorations

- Cover the tops of canopies with donated hay from local farmers.
- Ask floral shops for their throw-away greenery.
- Schools are oftentimes willing to provide decorations from their staging resources.
- Visit thrift stores and garage sales.
- If families and small groups volunteer and adopt a scene, they can bring decorations they already own, or they may be willing to purchase decorations for the church to keep.
- For a number of the storefronts, the owners will already have what they need; for example, the potter can bring his own potting wheel and items he already has made to outfit his shop.

Lighting

- Hold your event during daylight and avoid lighting issues altogether.
- If your event is indoors in your fellowship hall, multi-purpose room, gymnasium, or classroom, lighting will not be a problem.
- If you're holding your event outdoors, lighting becomes a bit trickier, but certainly solvable. Ask people from your congregation who work in construction or who camp; they might offer lighting services and expertise.

- Set up luminaries along outside walkways made with lunch-size paper bags, sand, and candles.
- Inexpensive, small spotlights or shop lights can be purchased at big box stores.
- Hang star-shaped Christmas lights throughout the area.
- WarnerPress.org/RecreatingChristmas-freeresources offers a free tutorial on how churches can create lighting that also mimics a campfire.
- Tiki torches are always an inexpensive option, but live fire can be a danger in public events. Proceed with caution.
- A simple online search yields other numerous, inexpensive lighting possibilities.

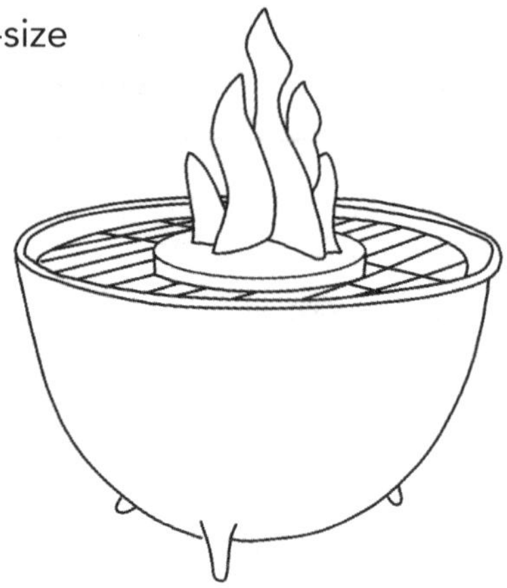

Kids' Activities

Most of the kids' activities are incorporated into Re-creating Christmas; however, a separate activity area can be set up for children to work on projects. Also, activities can be part of a take-home package for families.

- Ask a local woodworker to cut out ornaments from inexpensive wood.
- Purchase wooden clothes pins and have someone donate scrap pieces of fabric to make a clothespin nativity scene.
- Gather pine cones for students to paint or attach bird seed to.
- As a part of the food offerings, allow kids to decorate their own sugar cookies. Ask churchgoers or the high school family science department to bake sugar cookies and make frosting; purchase cookie decorations from a bulk store.
- Look online at WarnerPress.org/RecreatingChristmas-freeresources for free downloadable templates for more activities.

Food

- Purchase dry beans or lentils to make an inexpensive soup. Lentils were a readily available source of protein during Bible times. You can find a lentil soup recipe at WarnerPress.org/RecreatingChristmas-freeresources.
- Local grocery stores oftentimes will donate or sell items at a reduced price, when purchased in bulk.
- Naan bread, a seasoned flat bread, is fairly inexpensive to purchase or can be homemade.
- Like the kids' activities, some of the booths offer food such as bread, fruit, and cheese. Purchase these items in bulk or ask small groups or families to donate to the food fund.

- Oftentimes, the individuals in charge of a particular marketplace booth, cart, or storefront are willing to purchase their own supply of food they're "selling" at the outreach.

Advertising

Advertising just might be the biggest expense for your Christmas outreach, but this piece of the puzzle definitely should not be skimped on. Whether or not we want to admit it, in order for people to trust that your event will be excellent and worth coming to often is determined by the excellence of the communication behind Re-creating Christmas.

- Download free artwork for invitations, newspaper advertising, and posters at WarnerPress.org/RecreatingChristmas-freeresources for your outreach. The design work has been done for you; the only cost you incur is the printing cost.
- Equip volunteers with other ideas to reach out to visitors, as outlined in chapter 11.
- Leverage social media to get the word out.

So many people donate their time and energy! God just provides the people every year. Even people from other churches come in and help. I don't seek them out, but if they call and ask if they can have a part, we give them a part. It's been exciting to meet pastors who bring people from their churches to view the event as well.... One thing that has amazed me: when we started to do our event, it was to reach the unsaved. That was my main purpose, but it turns out, along with that, it has helped stabilize our church attendance, and the people inside our church have grown closer together....

It takes brilliance to pull off such an organizational feat. This is how I know without a doubt that this event is a work of God!

—Fran Emmons, GraceWay Bible Church, Hamilton, NJ

Chapter 4

Recruiting Volunteers: The Hands & Feet

People are so delighted to be a part of our [Christmas outreach]. They consider it a privilege to serve in this way.... Anyone who wants to celebrate Jesus' birthday can be involved. We have both costumed and non-costumed staff, ladies running the nursery or church kitchen. Some of the older people greet people coming into the church so they don't have to be outside.... Families or small groups will "adopt" a scene as their special investment. By far, this is the most efficient way because they will sign up year after year. Live drummers and live music are fabulous.

—Gayle Shriner, Discovery Baptist, Gig Harbor, WA

Love God. Love people.

These four words have the power to change everything. Our Savior calls it the greatest commandment:

> *"Love the Lord your God with all your heart and with all your soul and with all your mind." This is the first and greatest commandment. And the second is like it: "Love your neighbor as yourself."* —Matthew 22:37–39

Martin Luther King, Jr. also speaks about love that redeems and brings God's children together:

> *We must discover the power of love, the power, the redemptive power of love. And when we discover that, we will be able to make this old world a new world.... Love is the only way.*

When God's people really consider the implications of these words, and when they consider all Jesus did for them, they will want to reach out to others. They will want to share God's love to a hurting world. Because they have been redeemed, they will want to demonstrate this "redemptive power of love."

Love changes everything.

As you begin soliciting for volunteers, gently remind your church this is why we do what we do. They don't have to be actors or thespians to play certain roles—they just have to pretend, something we all did as children.

Approach this time with expectation. Pray that God will go ahead of you and stir hearts before you even ask for assistance. Sometimes we grow timid whenever we ask someone to sacrifice time or energy, but if you ask in believing, God will bring people to you. Ask as if eternity is at stake, because it is. Ask with joy and enthusiasm, and the response will be met with equal enthusiasm. You might also be surprised when people volunteer without your asking. They're ready and willing to help for the cause of Christ!

Growing the Team

After casting the vision and reminding others about the purpose of the outreach, grow the team.

Referencing the flow chart on page 28, the most ideal situation would be to petition individuals to be leaders for each area; in other words, ask one person to get volunteers to be characters and another person to oversee costumes. Ask an individual to oversee the food. Ask yet another individual to put together the crafts and activities areas. And ask a volunteer to oversee the building of the town of Bethlehem. Then each of those people find other volunteers to help.

The same would be true for hospitality and publicity. Ask that point person to seek a volunteer (or staff person, if someone is on staff who directs website content) to create the website and post on social media. Ask another individual to make copies of the downloaded posters and invitations. The hospitality and publicity director should also seek volunteers whose job on the day of the event simply is to help visitors feel at home and loved, from greeting them at the entrance of the event, to providing one final handshake when they leave.

If your church is smaller in size, some of these volunteers might need to pull double duty. For example, the individual who solicits volunteers to play certain character roles might be the same person who oversees costumes. The person overseeing hospitality and publicity might be the person who delivers posters throughout the neighborhood.

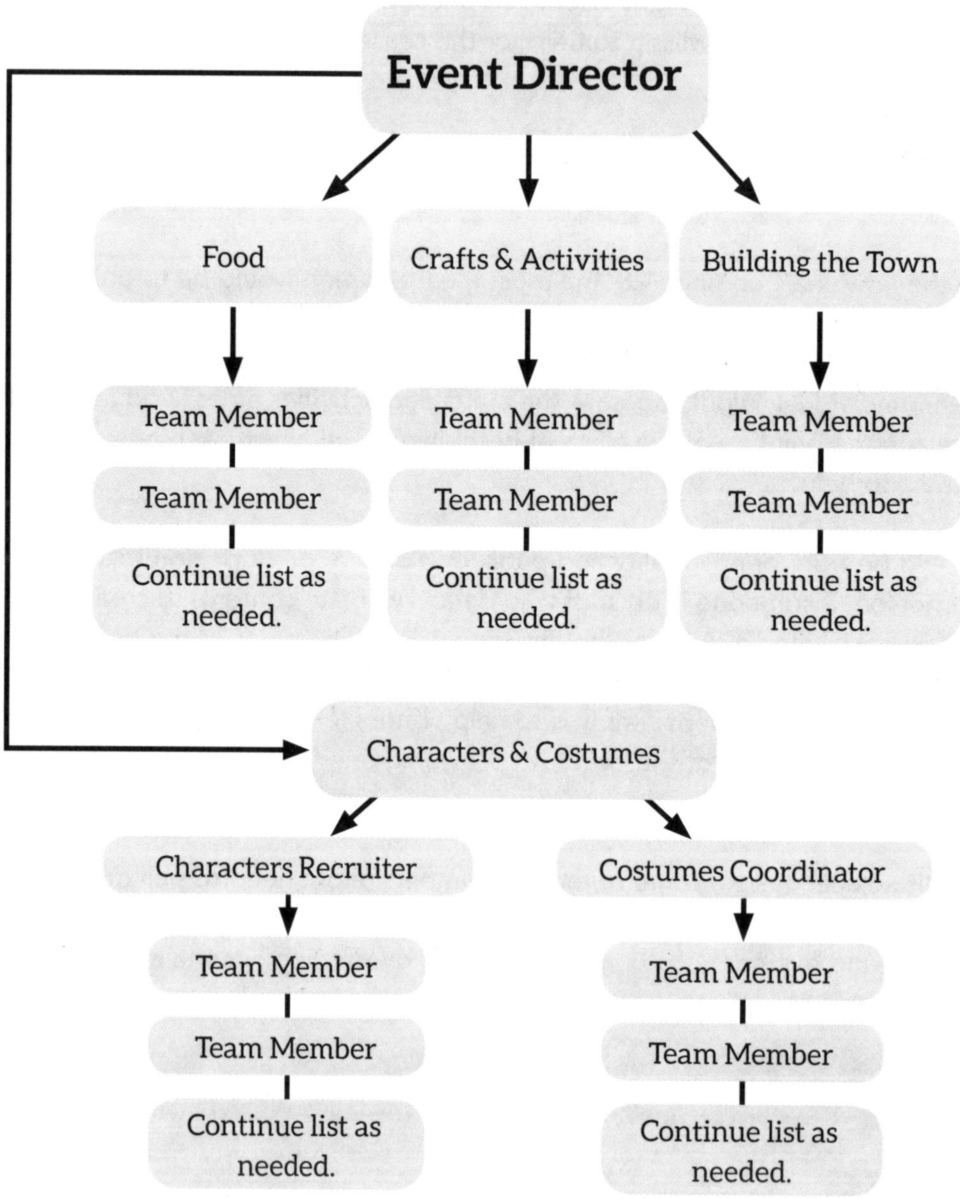
Event Director
Food
Crafts & Activities
Building the Town
Team Member
Team Member
Team Member
Team Member
Team Member
Team Member
Continue list as needed.
Continue list as needed.
Continue list as needed.
Characters & Costumes
Characters Recruiter
Costumes Coordinator
Team Member
Team Member
Team Member
Team Member
Continue list as needed.
Continue list as needed.

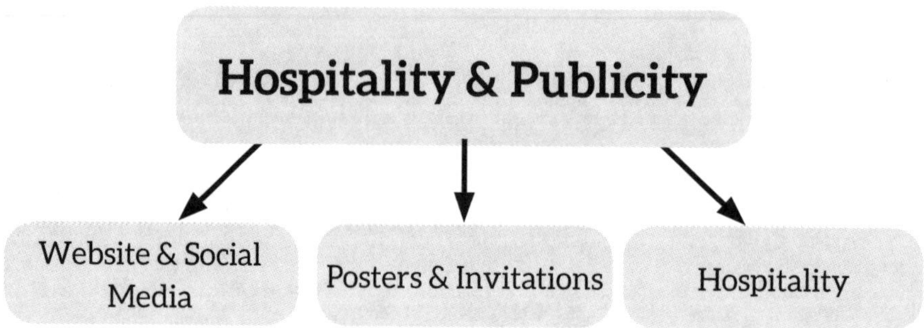
Hospitality & Publicity
Website & Social Media
Posters & Invitations
Hospitality

Choosing Volunteers

For many of us, we get stuck when we think about recruiting volunteers. Time is sacred in our world, and people are busy. Too busy.

At least that's what Satan wants us to think. Satan doesn't want us to ask for help. Satan wants us to believe people won't step up, because if people don't help, then the show can't go on, as they say.

But we know Satan is a liar. The reality is, many people in our congregation right now are more than willing to serve. They're ready to use their talents and gifts for Kingdom purposes. They may not necessarily want to work in the nursery for two months, but give them an opportunity to serve the community for an evening? They might be beyond eager.

After you have made needs known for volunteers, be sure your church knows what specific roles need filled. Need a handyman? You will find several. Need a seamstress? Sewing is becoming a lost art, but you'll find people who can fulfill this need. Need actors? Some people would look forward to losing the investment banker role and becoming a shepherd for an evening. Need someone to organize food? That retired school cook has organized food for hundreds of kids, so this should be a walk in the park by comparison.

Some people will step up right on their own. They will catch the vision and come to you. But there might come a time when you have to begin tapping others on the shoulder. Even though this might take a little more energy from you, pursue it with Kingdom energy. Some people simply don't have the imagination to see themselves in certain roles or even being helpful, but the second you ask, they will say yes. Maybe an entire small group would want to work together at a specific task. Ask an entire family to serve together. Ask the praise team to join efforts and do something together.

You might even want to look beyond the walls of your church. Look to local school drama classes or clubs. Look to area civic theaters. Look to other church youth groups or even adult groups. Get current volunteers to recruit their friends. For example, it's highly possible someone inside your church is friends with or related to a police officer who would make a great Roman soldier. A more radical thought is to invite a specialty volunteer who may not yet be a believer. Who knows? Involvement may be the perfect catalyst for this person to become a Christ-follower!

In particular, think about those amazing crafters, artisans, and small businesses who can help with the event. Your community might have a weaver, a jewelry maker, or even a potter. Maybe someone local sells fabulous spices or even specialty olive oils.

Here is a list of different groups to consider asking to volunteer:

- Women's ministry
- Men's ministry
- Sunday school groups
- Small groups (care groups, life groups)
- Service groups
- Elders and deacons
- Youth groups
- Local school groups
- Scouting or 4-H groups
- Civic theater
- College groups
- Singles group
- Young adult group
- Pastoral team
- Families
- Friends
- Praise team
- Local crafters and store owners

One more thing: for the most effective manger scene, recruit a family who are parents of a young baby. Where other gaps might not be filled in the volunteer pool or other concessions might need to be made along the way, families who attend the outreach need to come face to face with the reality that Jesus came as a real baby, God in the flesh. Seeing a Baby lying in a manger brings that truth home.

Staying Organized

Have a sign-up sheet ready to go on the Sunday the announcement is made about the Re-creating Christmas event. Make sure you get individuals' names, phone numbers, email addresses, and the role they would like to play. Include this information in your digital or printed spreadsheet. (Warner Press offers a complimentary spreadsheet online at WarnerPress.org/RecreatingChristmas-freeresources.)

You can also create a Google sheet or sign-up page on your church website where people can go online to sign up.

Staying organized is important, not only for recruiting volunteers, but also for communicating with them. Start with a thank you email or text. Keep it short and sweet. Remind them of their role and to mark their calendars now for the rehearsal and for the outreach. Tell them you're praying for them.

You don't have to approach recruitment with fear and trembling. Ask God to help you, to anoint this time, and He will.

> *I am the Lord's servant.* —Luke 1:38

> *Just as a body, though one, has many parts, but all its many parts form one body, so it is with Christ.... Now you are the body of Christ, and each one of you is a part of it.*
> —1 Corinthians 12:12, 27

I was not prepared for the impact [the Christmas outreach] would have on me as a volunteer. I work pretty far behind the scenes; I help prepare the food and the costumes. In learning about the food people ate during Bible times or learning about the significance of the types of clothes they wore, I have discovered this amazing story God was orchestrating all along. And then the non-Christians who attend, they're not exactly sure what they're getting into, but their curiosity brings them here, and they're exposed to this amazing reality of Christ coming for them! It's probably the greatest church event I participate in to help people come to know Christ.

—Donna, Volunteer

Chapter 5

Casting Characters: The People

> *Some people expect a hokey performance, and what they get is completely different, this reality.... They're mesmerized by the rabbis and floored by the wise men and shocked by the angels. They come back, and they bring friends, and they thank you, and they send gifts to the church. The payoff? What else could we possibly do on the mission field of reaching others for Christ? It has highly impacted our community.*
>
> —Gayle Shriner, Discovery Baptist Church, Gig Harbor, WA

The Christmas story is uncanny. An angel visits a young girl and tells her she will give birth to God.

She delivers that Baby in a stinky, dirty barn surrounded by cows, lambs, and a donkey. Then shepherds show up telling Mary and Joseph some angels visited them. Several years later, three men from a completely different part of the world come to visit and drop off some gifts.

Then there's Jesus Himself. God. God's Son. He was content in Heaven to enjoy relationship with the Father, but He also knew the time would come when He would leave perfection so someday we would know His perfection.

The story is so beyond our comprehension, it must have been written by Someone beyond our comprehension. It must have been written by God Himself and for a very important reason.

God wrote the story to save us:

> *God did not send his Son into the world to condemn the world, but to save the world through him.* —John 3:17

Now, we get to share that good news with others in Re-creating Christmas. We don't have to walk up to a stranger and ask, "If you died tonight, do you know where you would spend eternity?" We don't have to cite the four spiritual laws. We don't even have to talk about Jesus being the bridge that connects God to mankind. All of these methods are wonderful and have a specific purpose, but for many of us, the thought of engaging in these acts makes us wiggle with discomfort.

But we can don a costume, play the role of a character, and invite guests to step into the Christmas story.

This narrative goes well beyond Jesus, Mary, Joseph, shepherds, and the wise men. We find centuries-old prophecies in the Old Testament about Jesus. In the New Testament, other important characters are cast into the scenes. Even more, an entire culture sets the backdrop for Jesus' perfectly-timed arrival.

You might not be able to cast all the characters if you do not have enough actors, but it is important to have the key characters.

Primary Characters

- Mary
- Joseph
- Jesus
- Shepherds
- Wise Men
- Angel (who visits the shepherds)
- Innkeeper

Once these roles are filled, it's time to think about the volunteers who will create the town of Bethlehem as villagers, families, and shop owners. Scripts are provided in chapters six and seven. Feel free to choose as many of these characters as you can, depending upon your volunteer pool.

The Culture and Marketplace

- 1-3 Roman Soldiers
- Doctor and His Apothecary
- Baker
- Basket Maker
- Carpenter
- Potter
- Metal Shop Owner/Engraver
- Candy Maker
- Clothier
- Fisherman
- Rope Maker/Weaver
- Jewelry Store
- Olive Press
- Lamp Shop
- Scribe
- Spice Shop
- Food Shop Owners, including Fruits, Vegetables, and Cheese
- Villager (Part of Hospitality)

A third layer of characters include those individuals who appear in the biblical narrative. They are not necessarily critical to the event, but if your church has enough volunteers, they certainly add to the telling of the story.

Other Important Figures

- Isaiah
- Elizabeth and Zechariah
- King Herod
- Simeon
- Anna

Finally, if possible, include live animals, particularly lambs, a donkey, a cow, or maybe even a camel. A local farmer might be willing to set up a small petting area.

Getting into Character
Share with your volunteers the following information:

While you are in the city of Bethlehem and in costume, leave behind the 21st Century and enter Bethlehem AD 1. Stay in character 100% of the time. Many family, friends, and visitors will try to pull you out of character for a quick laugh but continue to remain in character. If guests ask questions about modern things, remember that you live in Bethlehem. Their terminology is confusing to you. Be polite but stay authentic to the time period. If you are a shopkeeper, study your trade and be prepared to explain it to the guests.

Create Your Name: If you are a shopkeeper or villager, come up with a Hebrew name and use that name for as long as you are in character. Try to memorize the names of the people in your shop or group.

Male names you can use:

Aaron
Abel
Abner
Abraham
Adam
Amos
Andrew
Benjamin
Boaz
Daniel
David
Eli
Elisha
Esau
Ezra
Gideon
Haman
Isaac
Ishmael
Jacob
James
Jesse
Joab
Joel
Jonah
Jonathan
Joseph
Joshua
Laban
Levi
Malachi
Matthew
Micah
Naaman
Reuben
Samson
Samuel
Simeon
Terah
Tobiah
Uriah
Zacharias
Zebadiah
Zebedee

Female names you can use:

Abigail
Abijah
Adah
Agar
Anah
Anna
Bernice
Candace
Deborah
Dinah
Elisabeth
Esther
Eunice
Eve
Hagar
Huldah
Iscah
Jemima
Jersha
Joanna
Judeth
Julia
Leah
Lydia
Mara
Martha
Mary
Michal
Miriam
Naomi
Orpah
Rachel
Rahab
Rhoda
Ruth
Sarah
Susanna
Tamar
Zillah
Zipporah

Develop a Story: Have a background. Are you married? If so, do you have children? How long have you practiced your trade? Who lives in your house? How many siblings do you have? How do you feel about the census? The more you become your character, the more convincing your portrayal will be.

If you are a shop owner, the other people in that shop are your family. Even if those in the shop are not your "real" family, portray yourselves as if you are a family.

Try to know the names of the people who work in the shops around you.

Generating Topics of Conversation

Political Talk: Roman rule is oppressive. Complain about high taxes from the Roman government. Express your dislike of the Roman soldiers but show fear when the soldiers are near. You may be interested in the "mood" of the Roman soldiers; their unwanted presence is a constant reminder that you are a "conquered" people.

Family Talk: Converse with other villagers, shopkeepers, and visitors about your families. Do you have a daughter or son about to be married? Do you have grandchildren? Is your mother ill? Does your husband work too hard? Talk about anything and everything related to family and culture!

Visitor Talk: The census has brought so many visitors to Bethlehem, there are many strangers you do not know. Ask them where they are from. Get to know them and welcome them to Bethlehem. Warn them to watch out for the Roman soldiers and the tax collector.

Religious Talk: This should be a very big part of your conversations since the purpose of Re-creating Christmas is to share about Jesus coming to our world. Let others know the rabbi is available for anyone who would like to be prayed for. Tell someone you need to purchase some doves for an offering. Share that your family is traveling to Jerusalem next week for the festival. Talk about the prophet you saw preaching out on the streets yesterday. However, avoid talking in "Christian" terms as your portrayal is before the birth of Christ. Don't talk about Jesus, any New Testament books, or the cross. Talk about the hope you have in the Messiah and refer to the Scriptures and the prophets.

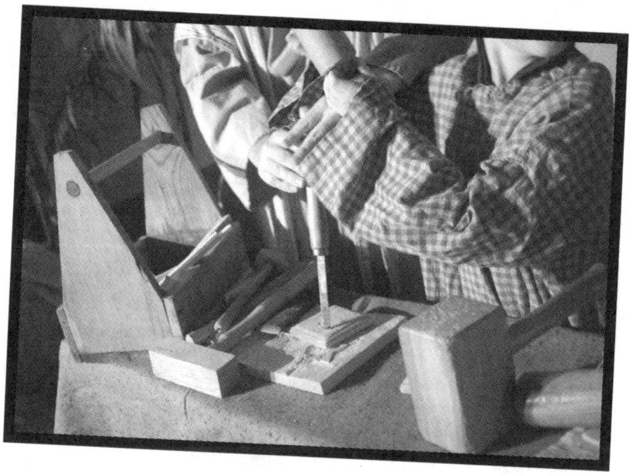

Initiating Shop Talk

If you are a shop owner, your livelihood depends on your sales, and your sales depend on convincing your customers that your merchandise is of superior quality. Is it an essential item for any home? How is your product useful? Does it provide warmth, light, and convenience? Is it a necessity of life? What will your product do? Why would anyone visit your shop and be interested in your merchandise? Is it attractive? Does it delight the eye, the touch? Will it hold something, or serve something? Is it a good buy? Is it unique? Have you worked hard in making this item? Is this a family business? How many generations of your family have been in this kind of business? Who taught you your trade? Explain your trade or craft and see if anyone is interested in buying or trading.

Another approach is to think of the purpose of your merchandise 2,000 years ago. Share that use with your visitors.

Rather than allowing them to walk by only looking at your product, initiate conversation. For example, if you sell baskets, tell visitors, "Our baskets are good for holding food items, linen items, wool for weaving, grain to be threshed, and beans to be cooked."

More importantly, get to know your guests by being personal. You will enjoy learning from them. Ask them about their travel and how they like Bethlehem. Ask if they had any trouble registering their family lineage.

When there are no visitors nearby, they are likely still watching you. Interact with those around you and continue practicing your trade.

Engaging Questions

While you want to be friendly and interact with the visitors, engage them only enough to feel welcome; you want them to experience all of Bethlehem. Also, always bring the conversation back around to the current situation, then bid them good day.

Sample Questions:

- Where have you come from?
    - What part of the Empire is…?
    - Is that east of Babylon?
    - Shepherdsville? Nice name. Maybe we should change our name to Shepherdsville. We have enough shepherds around here!
    - That sounds like beautiful country. I am not familiar with your city.
- Who is your governor? I have not heard of him. News travels slow around here.
- What is your trade? Where did you learn that from? Do you sell a lot of your items?
- Are your children apprentices? What do they do with their time? What types of chores do they do?
- You are not in tunics or robes. What are those nice garments you wear? Why do your sandals cover your whole foot? Is it cold where you are from? Is that why you are so bundled up?
- How did you travel here? What's a car? Do your feet hurt?
- Do you have relatives in Bethlehem?
- Just visiting? Why would you visit Bethlehem? If you want to visit a nice town, head over to Nazareth, or Genessaret. Those are nice towns.

Referencing Mary and Joseph

People are coming to Re-creating Christmas to see Baby Jesus. The more hints and gestures you can make about Mary and Joseph, the more these individuals will come to life. Mary and Joseph are not in the marketplace, so it's up to you to make it seem that the visitors just missed them.

For example, if you are a fisherman and own a fish shop, you might say, "The fish are extra good today. I had a young man and his wife stop in earlier for dinner. That girl ate four pieces of fish on her own! Of course, she was eating for two."

More sample scripts are provided in chapters 6 and 7.

Your character in this Christmas story reenactment is important! The role you play helps bring Bethlehem and the Christmas story into the 21st Century. For unbelieving or skeptical visitors, suddenly the notion of Jesus coming into the world as a Baby no longer feels mythical.

Invite the Holy Spirit into your preparation. Ask Him to help you with your role, and He will. With just a little effort, some imagination, and a lot of fun, you not only will be offering your guests an opportunity to imagine Bethlehem and the birth of Jesus as a real, life-changing event, you might just experience it in a deeper, more meaningful way for yourself!

> *Prepare the way for the* LORD*.... And the glory of the* LORD *will be revealed, and all people will see it together.* —Isaiah 40:3–5

> *This is our 41st year in performing [our Christmas outreach]. Each year we might have a few new people as characters, but we have some people who have done it for a long time. They take real ownership of the part they play...and they derive a real spiritual blessing.*
> —Steve DeLisle, Pastor, Maple Grove Church of God, Anderson, IN

Chapter 6

Supplying Scripts: The Key Characters' Words

The hardest part of recruiting is finding men who will do the speaking parts, specifically the rabbis and wise men, because we script those parts. Other guys are more than willing to be out and about holding sheep. They like being centurions, too.

—Gayle Shriner, Discovery Baptist Church, Gig Harbor, WA

The scripts provided in this chapter are fairly informal and are meant to be a guide, as they touch upon ways you can reflect the historical nature of Bethlehem. The primary characters and other important figures are represented in the Bible, so your actors might choose to quote or paraphrase Scripture passages. They don't need to memorize the verses; they can simply talk as they would to a friend or neighbor.

Encourage your characters to explore the biblical narrative, especially Luke 2, in a variety of translations or paraphrases in order to get a good understanding of their role. In particular, *The Voice* is a great paraphrase, as this Bible version is compiled by writers, musicians, poets, and other artists, alongside scholars and pastors.

> *Don't be afraid! Listen! I bring good news, news of great joy, news that will affect all people everywhere. Today, in the city of David, a Liberator has been born for you! He is the promised Anointed One, the Supreme Authority! You will know you have found Him when you see a baby, wrapped in a blanket, lying in a feeding trough.* —Luke 2:10–12 (VOICE)

The Primary Characters

These characters are central to the Christmas story, so make sure they are front and center in your outreach. Your church should assign each of these significant people their own "room," or staging area, to provide the scenes for the Christmas story. Consider staging them in the order of the scripts.

The next chapter offers more information on other cast members and their roles to bring Bethlehem to life. Chapter 9 is dedicated to ideas on staging.

The Innkeeper
The innkeeper appears first. He stands by a home or small building, a lamp, a door, and maybe some sort of tree.

Bible Reference: Luke 2:7

Innkeeper Sample Script:
"I'm sorry we don't have any room for you. We've been so busy with the census travelers. I'm feeling great about all this business, except I feel bad for that young couple that was about to have a baby. I'd have given them my own bed if I hadn't already sold it to someone else!"

"I am very tired today. A bright light kept me awake all night! Funny thing, it appeared in the sky soon after I had to turn away that nice man and his pregnant wife. Did you see them? I wonder if they're okay?"

Angel (who visits the shepherds) & Heavenly Host
The angel appears second, and if you have enough volunteers, you can also have a host of angels who stroll throughout the village proclaiming the Baby's arrival.

Bible Reference: Luke 2:9–14

Angel Sample Script:
"Are you from around here? I'm from another world (laugh), literally. I had to deliver a message to some ragamuffin shepherds, but it was good news of great joy! I didn't mean to, but I think I scared them. Funny thing, I had to give them directions even though I hadn't been to the manger myself yet (laughs again)! I tell ya, you just gotta have a sense of humor in my line of work."

Heavenly Host Sample Script:
"Glory to God in the Highest!"
"Peace and goodwill to all!"
"Praise God!"
"A Savior has been born!"

Shepherds
These simple, agrarian fellows appear third on the scene. Ideally, you might try having one or two shepherds in a staged area who talk about the angels' appearance. If you have enough volunteers, you also can have shepherds strolling through the village.

Bible Reference: Luke 2:8–20

"Staged" Shepherds Sample Script:
"We were just doing what we normally do, guarding our flock of sheep from predatory animals, and from out of nowhere, this… angel, I guess, appeared! Scared us to death at first, until it told us not to be afraid. Then we were told about the Messiah being born. We thought it was crazy—until we found out for ourselves! Mind-blowing."

Village Shepherds Sample Script:
"Have you seen them?! We were the first visitors there! The angel told us a Baby would be wrapped in cloths and lying in a manger. That's exactly what we saw! Amazing!"

Wise Men
Wise men were scholars who knew Old Testament prophecy. They also studied natural signs, including the stars, to help them interpret the world around them.

Stage three magi, or wise men, in a fourth area, holding ornate gift packages and standing near a desk or table piled with scrolls.

Bible Reference: Matthew 2:1–16

Wise Men Sample Script:
"We were peering out at the night sky, and a glorious star appeared. We knew immediately this was a sign telling us the King of the Jews had been born!"

"First, we traveled from the East and asked Herod where we would find the Newborn King. That Herod is a very bad man. We don't trust him. But that star led us right to the Messiah. It has been an exciting, holy journey."

"We brought this Baby three gifts. Gold…for the King of kings. Frankincense…for the Priest of all priests. And Myrrh…to honor the sacrifice this Baby will offer someday."

Mary, Joseph, and Jesus

The last central figures to the story are the most obvious: Baby Jesus and His parents. They should appear in a barn or cave-like setting with a wooden trough holding hay.

Reference: Matthew 1—2; Luke 1—2

Joseph Sample Script:

"An angel appeared to me in a dream and told me to name the Baby 'Jesus,' which means, 'The Lord Saves.' All this happened just as we were told: Mary would come with me to Bethlehem. Jesus would be born here. We would have visitors, and the shepherds and wise men visited. God's hand truly is upon us."

Mary Sample Script:

"It's so strange to think this Child I carried is also my Lord. Those tiny hands and feet will someday rule the world. I can touch the face of God in this precious Baby. He seems so normal, like you and me. He is my son, and He is also the Son of God. My soul magnifies the Lord!"

Jesus

Try to use a real baby to portray Jesus. Doing so will show the visitors the Son of God was like every other baby who cried, slept, messed his diaper, and interacted with his parents.

Other Important Figures

If you have the volunteer capacity and after you have garnered volunteers for the town of Bethlehem, you can add another layer of people to Re-creating Christmas. From an Old Testament prophet to a ruthless ruler and even Mary's cousin, these individuals appear as the biblical narrative unfolds.

Isaiah

God instructs Isaiah to prophecy, or tell the Jewish people, that they will someday have a Savior.

References: Isaiah 40:3–5; Isaiah 7:14; Isaiah 61:1; and Isaiah 52:13–53:12

Isaiah Sample Script:

"I lived 700 years before Jesus, but God Almighty told me about Christ's birth. I shared that Good News with the people of Judah. They had turned away from the true God. I hoped that by learning about the coming of the Messiah, they would change their ways. Indeed, they did turn back to God, but sadly, it was only temporary."

Another approach to Isaiah's character is to have this person prophecy throughout your town:

"The Spirit of the Lord is on me to bring good news and help repair broken hearts! Be free from your prison of sin! The glory of the Lord will be revealed! The Lord has spoken! A young maiden will conceive. She will give birth to a son and name Him Immanuel. By His stripes we are healed!"

Elizabeth and Zechariah

Elizabeth is Mary's cousin; Zechariah and she are John the Baptist's parents. Zechariah also was a priest.

Reference: Luke 1

Elizabeth Sample Script:

"I lived with disgrace for so long because I could not have a baby. Then God blessed us with a child! While I was carrying him, Cousin Mary visited, and my baby leapt in my womb! I knew then both Mary and the baby were blessed by God."

Zechariah Sample Script:

"God sent the angel Gabriel to tell me we would have a son, but because I didn't believe, I could not talk until after our baby was born. After I proclaimed his name would be John, my voice was miraculously restored. Everyone knew John was blessed by God. My son became a prophet for the coming of the Messiah! He prepared the way for the Lord!"

Herod

Herod was the King of Judea and was a cruel, vindictive man. He was intimidated by the so-called King of the Jews who had been born, so he set out to try to kill the Baby Jesus. But as with any God-ordained moment, Herod's plans were thwarted.

Reference: Luke 1:5; Matthew 2

Herod Sample Script:

"I am so nervous about that Baby Boy being born! They call Him a King, but *I* am king! Those not-so-wise men told me about the Baby; I told them after they found Him to come back and tell me where He is so I could go worship, too, but they didn't! I have to find that Baby! He cannot rule because I am King Herod!!"

Simeon

Simeon loved the Lord; his heart was sensitive to the Truth of God. He anticipated Jesus' arrival would bring help for the Jewish people.

Reference: Luke 2:25–35

Simeon Sample Script:

"God Almighty informed me I would not die before I saw the Anointed One. I am an old man who is ready to be with God, and now I hear the Messiah has arrived! He will set us free by losing His life. He is the Light to all! Hallelujah!"

Anna

Anna was an 84-year-old prophetess who loved God. She was deeply devoted to the Lord, spending her time in the temple, fasting and praying.

Reference: Luke 2:36–38

Anna Sample Script:

"Thanks to God, the Messiah has come! Hope is born! Jerusalem is rescued from oppression! Have you seen the Lord yet? If you see Him, will you ask His parents to bring Him to the temple? I cannot wait to see our Savior! Quick, go look for Him so you can celebrate, too!"

> *One mom shared with me her son had stopped going to church—he wasn't sure he even believed in God anymore. But he came to the outreach with us, and later he told them his faith had been restored because of [our Christmas outreach].*
>
> —Name Withheld, Volunteer

Chapter 7

Bringing Life: The Town and Villagers

We assemble a hybrid of shops, and the important thing is that the town is biblically-based.... We create a town bakery where we offer snacks to the guests.... A special moment comes near the end at the manger scene. This bright star comes on, the little kids see Baby Jesus, and they just storm the manger. That's definitely a highlight.
—Kimberly Tussing, Children's Ministry Director, Mountain Park Church, Phoenix, AZ

You've seen them. Maybe you even know them or are one of them: local storeowners with a specific niche market and whose livelihoods depend upon courtesy, customer service, and selling their wares. Someone at the farmer's market sells honey. An acquaintance opens his own pottery shop. The hardware store down the street sells tools on one side and candy on the other side.

Town centers often generate a love and energy for their citizens, and this same feeling would have been no different 2,000 years ago in the town of Bethlehem.

> *On the plains of Moab by the Jordan across from Jericho, the LORD said to Moses, "Command the Israelites to give the Levites towns to live in from the inheritance the Israelites will possess. And give them pasturelands around the towns. Then they will have towns to live in and pasturelands for the cattle they own and all their other animals.... Six of the towns you give the Levites will be cities of refuge."* —Numbers 35:1–3, 6

> *Soon afterward, Jesus went to a town called Nain, and his disciples and a large crowd went along with him.* —Luke 7:11

A central component of Re-creating Christmas includes those people who make up the town of Bethlehem. Choose any or all of these individuals listed throughout this chapter to make up your 2,000-year-old community that's home to the Christ Child. If your church is low on volunteers, no worries! Simply choose from the list of shop owners.

The villagers make your visitors feel welcome, as if they are a part of Bethlehem, and that they belong. Through their realistic portrayal of common Bethlehem citizens, these people reenact the hustle and bustle of first century life.

Their roles are especially important because they extend hospitality toward the guests, those attending Re-creating Christmas. A great interaction with a visitor might translate into that visitor's choosing to return to your church.

Villagers will find themselves:

- choosing a Bible name for their character (see chapter 5)
- inviting guests to explore the marketplace
- inviting guests to interact with the villagers
- calling other villagers/shopkeepers by their names, and
- becoming excited about the birth of the Messiah

Chapter 5 provides a general look at the villagers' roles. This chapter offers more detail, but along with memorizing a statement or two, encourage villagers just to be themselves, relax, and improvise.

Imagine a first century marketplace similar to today's outdoor farmer or craft markets. People set up their booths, or storefronts, throughout town. They try to sell their goods, interact with the visitors, and help them feel welcome.

Shop owners knew how to sell their items. They were experts about their merchandise because they dedicated their lives to producing and/or selling it. Therefore, they were always smiling and willing to talk to anyone to make a deal.

Shops & Food Cart Information

People love to eat today, and that was no different in Bethlehem:

> *He makes grass grow for the cattle, and plants for people to cultivate—bringing forth food from the earth.* —Psalm 104:14
>
> *He provides food for those who fear him; he remembers his covenant forever.* —Psalm 111:5
>
> *The generous will themselves be blessed, for they share their food with the poor.* —Proverbs 22:9

Food not only was used for sustenance and fuel, it also was an opportunity to show hospitality. The people of Bethlehem had several types of food in their diet; they certainly didn't live off of bread and water alone!

Families oftentimes would sell handmade goods and food from their homes. Other times, they might have small open-air booths set up similar to what we might see at an outdoor swap meet or flea market today. Activity surrounded both the homes and the markets.

For your outreach, set up carts and booths in a variety of places. If your church is small, set them up in your fellowship hall. If the weather is nice, scatter carts and booths around outside. Decorate them with fruits and vegetables, honey, jewelry, leather goods, and woven baskets.

Special Note:

The following pages offer ideas and short sample scripts for recreating a bustling Bethlehem with its shops and food carts. Feel free to offer these individual pages to your church volunteers who will be playing these roles. Upon reading, they will quickly imagine what their places for selling their goods or food can look like.

Bread Shop Information

Bread was a staple part of the Jewish diet and it was baked fresh daily. It was such a central part of the diet that the common phrase, "to break bread," referred to eating a full meal.

> *On the first day of the week we came together to break bread.* —Acts 20:7

Wheat was the grain of choice for making bread. Barley was also used, but it was not preferred and was therefore reserved mostly for the poor. A baker would have baked her bread from scratch. She would grind the grain—either wheat or barley—and then she would add water, season it with salt, and add some leavening if desired.

Leaven was a small amount of dough that had been saved from the previous day's batch of bread. The dough was kneaded and given time to rise. Bread was not baked in bread or loaf pans. Instead, it was pressed into small discs.

Unleavened bread was baked and because it didn't rise, the round bread could be wrapped around other foods. It was also used in the place of spoons to scoop up parts of the meal.

Bakers didn't have ovens as we know of ovens today. The wealthy had ovens made of brick. A fire would be lit inside, and the dough would be stuck to the walls to allow it to bake. If you were without an oven, the most common way to bake bread was to dig a hole in the ground and build a fire in the hole.

Sample Baker Script:
"You can smell the aroma of my bread throughout the entire village! People flock to my shop! Because of the census, I haven't been able to keep up with the demand! A nice man and his wife stopped by last night when I had a few scraps to share. I was glad to do it; that poor girl looked so tired, and her husband looked worried!"

What to Do When Someone Visits Your Shop

- Share small samples of your bread with your visitors.
- Educate your guests on the facts of bread in Bethlehem. The name "Bethlehem" means "House of the Bread."

Fish Market Information

Right from the very beginning, the Lord blessed the occupation of a fisherman:

> *Then God said, "Let us make mankind in our image, in our likeness, so that they may rule over the fish in the sea and the birds in the sky, over the livestock and all the wild animals, and over all the creatures that move along the ground."* —Genesis 1:26

Fishing was a common occupation. Rods and reels utilizing hooks and bait were not used. Instead, fishing was done using nets.

DRAGNET

This was an enormous net that measured about 100 feet long and 12 feet high. Ropes were attached to both ends and sinkers were used to weight the bottom. Two teams were used to cast the net and drag it in. One team went out while another stayed and anchored the net. The net was maneuvered into a large circle and then dragged ashore.

CAST NET

This circular net was about 20 feet in diameter and had weights secured to the bottom edge. This net could be used from a boat or from the shore. If thrown correctly, the net would hit the water as an open circle and then sink to the bottom, trapping fish under it like a parachute. After casting, the fisherman had to dive into the water and carefully pull the bottom of the net together and then out.

TRAMMEL NET

This net was actually three nets in one. Two of the nets formed walls while the middle net was finer and helped entangle the fish. The net, once assembled, was dragged into a circle, trapping fish inside.

Since refrigeration was not available, fish were packed in salt to preserve their freshness.

There were at least 23 varieties of fish in the Sea of Galilee. These were preserved and brought all the way to the markets in towns like Bethlehem. No fish would have been found in the Dead Sea.

Sample Fisherman Script:
"We were very fortunate to have caught so many fish this morning. The fish are extra good today, too. I had a young man and his wife stop in earlier for dinner. That girl ate four on her own. Of course, she was eating for two."

What to Do When Someone Visits Your Shop

- Educate your guests on where and how the fish were caught.

Candy Maker Information

It is clear in the Bible that people have always liked eating candy and sweets!

But Jonathan had not heard that his father had bound the people with the oath, so he reached out the end of the staff that was in his hand and dipped it into the honeycomb. He raised his hand to his mouth, and his eyes brightened. —1 Samuel 14:27

When you're given a box of candy, don't gulp it all down; eat too much chocolate and you'll make yourself sick. —Proverbs 25:16 (MSG)

Since sugar was not readily available, candies were made of dates, honey, almonds, pistachios, butter, corn syrup, and gum base. These early candy makers mixed the ingredients to produce sweetness of a definite flavor, texture, and color. They shaped the candy by spinning or by rolling it into strips ready for cutting.

It was quite common for people to nibble on sweets during and between meals.

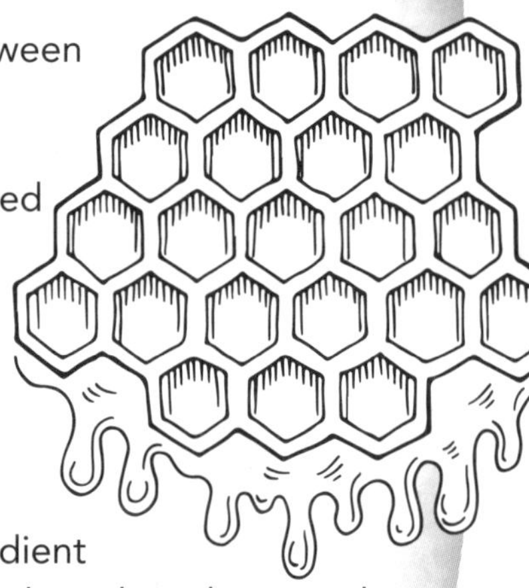

The royal family and the very rich were supplied with dainties prepared by experts.

HONEY: Since there was no sugar in Israel, honey was the main sweetener. Did you know that the Jewish Scriptures (our modern Old Testament) refer to honey more than 50 times?

ALMONDS: Still a delicacy today, the almond is not only a key ingredient in sweets, it was also used to make very expensive oil. Did you know that when the rod of Aaron sprouted, it bore almonds (Numbers 17:8)? *Although almonds were a central part of the Bethlehem culture food supplies, you might choose to omit this food source in your created town, given today's nut allergies in younger children.

GRAPES: Grapes were used for making wine, raisins, and grape syrup. Grape syrup is made by boiling grape juice until it reaches the consistency of molasses. It was sometimes called honey because of its thickness and sweet flavor.

Sample Candy Maker Script:
"I gave some grapes to that tiny young lady who seemed to be in much discomfort. I think she said her name is Mary. She was so grateful, and it seemed to ease her pain for a little while, so I gave her a few more to take with her. We grow the sweetest grapes around!"

What to Do When Someone Visits Your Shop
- Allow them to stir the ingredients to help you make candy.
- Provide samples of your candy (fudge) and ask their opinion.
- Educate them on the ingredients and the art of making candy.

Fruits & Vegetables Shop Information

The Bible contains numerous references about fruits and vegetables. Whether spoken about literally or spiritually, it is obvious these food groups are important for an individual's well-being.

> *Blessed is the one…whose delight is in the law of the* Lord*…. That person is like a tree planted by streams of water, which yields its fruit in season.* —Psalm 1:1–3

> *We remember the fish we ate in Egypt at no cost—also the cucumbers, melons, leeks, onions and garlic.* —Numbers 11:5

> *Better a small serving of vegetables with love than a fattened calf with hatred.* —Proverbs 15:17

> *Daniel then said…"Please test your servants for ten days: Give us nothing but vegetables to eat and water to drink."* —Daniel 1:11–12

FRUITS: Grapes and raisins were quite popular due to a perfect grape-growing climate. Grapes could only be eaten fresh during the harvest. Most were pressed to make wine or set out to dry for raisins. The spies who checked out the Promised Land brought back grapes the size of plums! Figs also were plentiful and were available ripe only for a short time. Figs were strung together and hung up to dry. Citrus fruits were just becoming available. Oranges, lemons, and limes were all grown along the coastal area. Because it was new, citrus was quite a delicacy! Other fruits included pomegranates, olives, and dates.

VEGETABLES: Beans were common, but the common bean was typically eaten only by the poor. Garbanzo beans could be toasted over a fire for a crunchy snack. Israelites loved cucumbers, garlic, and onions. Vegetables were in such demand that gardeners would set up guard towers to watch over their crop and protect against thieves.

Sample Fruit/Vegetable Grower Script:
"Praise God, He helps us grow such lovely produce! The soil is rich and fertile. We gave extra helpings to that young couple who came through several hours ago. They looked as if they had traveled for days! And the wife, she was being brave not to show her physical discomfort."

What to Do When Someone Visits Your Shop

- Educate them on the reasons we eat vegetables and what types of vegetables were available.
- Allow guests to enjoy a sampling of fruits and vegetables.

Meat and Cheese Shop Information

The Bible contains several discussions both in the Old and New Testaments about meat being consumed. Whether at a celebration or simply for sustenance, meat has a place in the biblical narrative.

> *The father said..., "Bring the fattened calf and kill it. Let's have a feast and celebrate. For this son of mine was dead and is alive again; he was lost and is found." So they began to celebrate.* —Luke 15:22–24

> *Whoever eats meat does so to the Lord, for they give thanks to God; and whoever abstains does so to the Lord and gives thanks to God.* —Romans 14:6

Meat was very expensive and reserved only for special occasions. Sheep, lambs, goats, fattened calves, gazelle, antelope, deer, doves, and quail were all eaten. Swine were available, too, but not for Hebrews. Milk from goats and cattle was used to make cheese. Cheese could be mixed with water to make a sour but cooling drink.

Sample Meat and Cheese Shop Script:
"We have some delicious, juicy meats here for you. And cheese! This cheese came from my favorite goat, Anna. She loves to share with others. She took a special liking to the girl who was here earlier. Her husband and she traveled all the way from Nazareth, in Galilee!"

What to Do When Someone Visits Your Shop

- Educate them on when meat was eaten and the types of meats and cheeses that were available.
- Allow guests to enjoy a sampling of meats and cheeses.

Olive Press & Olive Shop Information

Whether eaten for food or pressed for oil, olives were used for various reasons and were one of the most important crops in all of Israel. You will find many references in the Bible about this specific food.

> *Command the Israelites to bring you clear oil of pressed olives for the light so that the lamps may be kept burning.* —Exodus 27:20

> *When you beat the olives from your trees, do not go over the branches a second time. Leave what remains for the foreigner, the fatherless and the widow.* —Deuteronomy 24:20

The olive tree resembles an apple tree, and its flowers look like lilacs. Olives are green first, then change to black as they ripen. Though some olives were eaten fresh, and others pickled, the majority were pressed for oil. First the olives were heated to allow the oil to flow more readily. Olive oil was made by pressing with a stone or stomping the olives (typically the green ones). After the first and purest batch of oil was squeezed from the olive, the pulp would be taken and placed in a press created from large stones. The stones were rolled over the olives to produce cloudier, lower grade oil. The crop from one olive tree produced about 20 gallons of oil!

Olive oil was used for a multitude of things in everyday life. Some common uses included cooking, burning as a fuel in lamps, soap, make-up (made skin and hair healthy and shiny), anointing, and leather preservative.

Sample Olive Shop Script:
"We have some delicious, juicy olives here for you. And oh, you will love the oil for your food *and* for your lamps! See, it's very pure and will burn clean. This was all freshly pressed this morning."

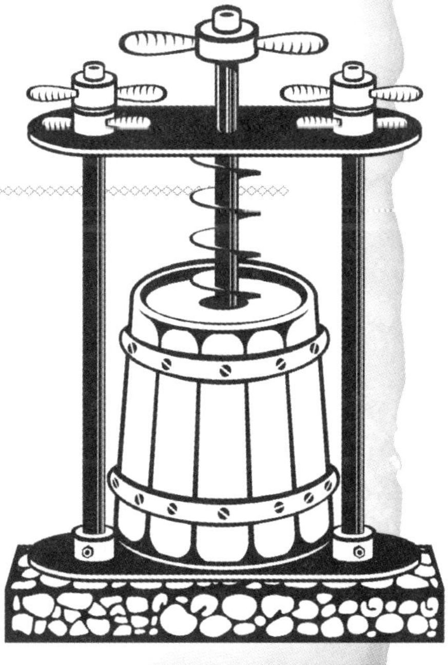

What to Do When Someone Visits Your Shop

- Educate them on why you press olives for oil and invite them to help press the olives.
- Allow guests to enjoy a sampling of different kinds of olives.

Spice Shop Information

Spices were used for enhancing the flavor of foods, for offering improved fragrance, for healing, and in caring for deceased bodies. Certain spices were available only to the wealthy. Spices sometimes carried a spiritual connotation.

> *Woe to you Pharisees, because you give God a tenth of your mint, rue and all other kinds of garden herbs, but you neglect justice and the love of God.* —Luke 11:42
>
> *Then they opened their treasures and presented him with gifts of…frankincense and myrrh.* —Matthew 2:11
>
> *My spikenard sends forth its fragrance.* —Song of Solomon 1:12 (NKJV)

The primary flavoring agent was salt, available in endless supply in the salt hills near the Dead Sea.

The land around Bethlehem was filled with strong herbs and spices. Spices that weren't available nearby were imported from India and Africa.

Caraway, dill, mint, mustard, parsley, sage, and thyme were all used freely for seasoning food.

Spices like frankincense and myrrh were actually made by crushing the hardened sap from trees. These two spices were also very expensive.

Lavender also has biblical roots. It is referred to as spikenard in some Bible versions and nard in other versions.

Sample Spice Shop Script:
"We have the best salt for your foods, and our lavender is so fragrant! I gave some lavender to that young girl and her husband. She will enjoy wrapping her Baby's blanket in its fragrance once the little One is born…which could be any time now, from the way she looked, Yahweh be with her."

What to Do When Someone Visits Your Shop

- Allow visitors to smell and feel the various spices. They can help by crushing the spices.
- Visitors can make a lavender sachet to take with them. Make squares of fabric and twine available.

Engraver Shop Information

Most biblical references to engravings and carvings are negative. Idol worship started with the creation of stone images carved by a skilled craftsman. There are several positive references, however, to show how the skill could be used for God's glory.

> *Engrave the names of the sons of Israel on the two stones the way a gem cutter engraves a seal. Then mount the stones in gold filigree settings.* —Exodus 28:11

> *He engraved cherubim, lions and palm trees on the surfaces of the supports and on the panels, in every available space, with wreaths all around.* —1 Kings 7:36

Engraving was a highly specialized skill. Wood, ivory, metal, and leather were all engraved to add a special touch. Chisels, punches, and hammers were tools that were used to carve the materials. The engraving tool could be a reed stylus, metal chisel, or flint point.

Sample Engraver Shop Script:
"I gave a special engraving to the young carpenter and his wife so they can give it to their Baby someday. Who knows? Maybe that Baby will be inspired to use tools as well?"

What to Do When Someone Visits Your Shop

- Ask visitors to help you engrave items.
- Use the various tools and watch children especially closely.

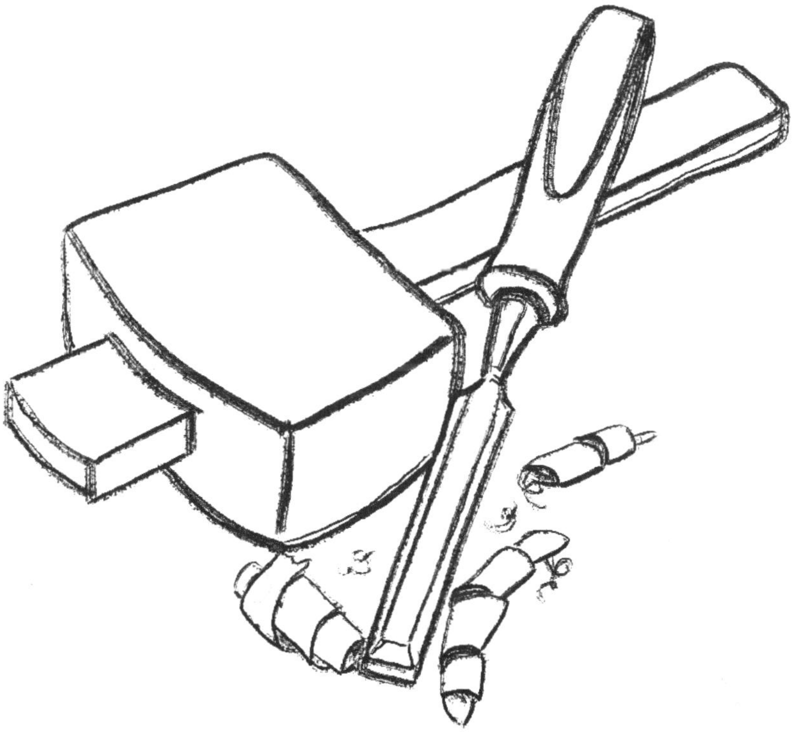

Lamp Shop Information

Candles were not yet invented during the time of Christ's birth; instead, homes and shops would mold a piece of pottery to hold olive oil and a wick.

> *There were many lamps in the upstairs room where we were meeting.* —Acts 20:8
>
> *Moses…set up the lamps before the* L*ORD*, *as the* L*ORD commanded him.*
> —Exodus 40:22, 25
>
> *You,* L*ORD*, *keep my lamp burning; my God turns my darkness into light.*
> *—Psalm 18:28*

The people were not afraid of the dark, but to sleep in the dark was a sign of poverty. A typical family would leave a lamp lit throughout the night.

Olive oil was used as a fuel in lamps, so you might want to place the lamp shop in close enough proximity to the olive shop so that the two owners can banter back and forth.

Lamp Shop Sample Script:
"Welcome to my shop, my friend! Everyone needs a good lamp so they can see at night. I have made enough to help many people who have come to be part of the census. I actually gave one to a young couple so they could make their way to the innkeeper's stable. The path there is especially difficult to traverse, and that poor couple looked like they needed some extra help."

What to Do When Someone Visits Your Shop
- Educate them on the process of making lamps.
- Allow them to assist you in creating lamps.

Pottery Shop Information

The work of the potter is used in the Bible to illustrate our relationship with the Lord. Just as a potter can manipulate a clump of clay into a beautiful vessel, so God wants His people to be moldable in His hands.

> *"Can I not do with you, Israel, as this potter does?" declares the* L*ORD*. *"Like clay in the hand of the potter, so are you in my hand, Israel.* —Jeremiah 18:6

> *Yet you,* L*ORD*, *are our Father. We are the clay, you are the potter; we are all the work of your hand.* —Isaiah 64:8

After clay had been gathered from nearby fields, it was brought to the potter's shop. It would be left in the sun long enough that worms and insects would crawl out. The potter would then trample the clay with his bare feet while adding water to bring it to just the right consistency.

When making items out of clay, three main methods were used. The potter often used molds to make common items like lamps. Shaping the clay freehand was primarily used in the creation of toys and of some kinds of ovens. The most common method (and the most fun) was to use the wheel. The foot-powered wheel was a very recent invention at the time. Previously, the potter had to turn the wheel by hand.

After the clay is formed into the desired shape, the potter had the option of decorating it. Sometimes the item would be "painted" with a thinned-down clay of another color. A common design was to paint a single stripe of red or black around the middle of the jar. It was also common to imprint the object with assorted instruments. It could be scratched with another piece of clay or imprinted with an item such as a woven rope.

Perhaps the two most difficult parts of a potter's job were getting the clay to the right consistency and correctly firing the objects in a kiln. Each type of clay needed to be fired at a different temperature. It wasn't as simple as turning up the thermostat, either. The heat was controlled by adding more wood and air to the fire.

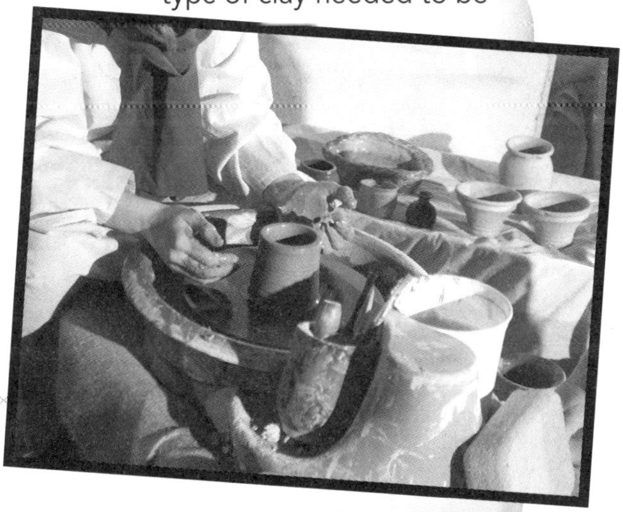

Sample Pottery Shop Script:
"We've sold quite a bit of merchandise today. I just had a young man come by to purchase a couple of water jugs. Sounds like his wife is having a baby. Heh…I bet that will throw their census numbers off!"

What to Do When Someone Visits Your Shop
- Encourage visitors to mold some of your clay.
- Explain some details about your art.

Basket Maker Information

Probably the most well-known Bible story involving the use of a basket has to do with Moses when he was a baby.

> *When she could hide him no longer, she got a papyrus basket for him and coated it with tar and pitch. Then she placed the child in it and put it among the reeds along the bank of the Nile.* —Exodus 2:3

Another popular mention of baskets is found in the feeding of the 5,000.

> *The disciples picked up twelve basketfuls of broken pieces of bread and fish.* —Mark 6:43

Baskets were made of various materials and in different shapes and sizes. They typically were plaited or woven. They would be used to carry fruit, bread, cakes, and clay. Additionally, they could be used to store things like grain.

The large, deep basket referred to in Deuteronomy 26:2, 4, was a common household article, along with the kneading trough. Shaped like a jar, it was used for storing grain, which is poured in at the top and removed as needed from an opening at the bottom.

> *Take some of the firstfruits of all that you produce from the soil of the land the LORD your God is giving you and put them in a basket. Then go to the place the LORD your God will choose as a dwelling for his Name…. The priest shall take the basket from your hands and set it down in front of the altar of the LORD your God.*
> Deuteronomy 26:2, 4

Besides baskets, the reeds and grasses could be used to make a number of other items. A good basket maker could make hampers, mats, and ropes.

Sample Basket Shop Script:
"I had a really nice basket earlier that I would have loved to show you. Where did it…oh that's right, I sold it to that young girl and her husband. Poor child, she had been riding all day on a donkey. I hope she is not too tired."

What to Do When Someone Visits Your Shop
- Try to convince your guests they need your baskets.
- Allow guests to assist you in weaving some of the partially finished baskets.

Carpenter and Metal Shop Information

The most famous carpenters in the Bible were Jesus and His earthly father, Joseph. However, numerous places in the Bible refer to carpentry:

> *And the LORD showed me four carpenters.* —Zechariah 1:20 (KJV)
>
> *The carpenter measures with a line and makes an outline with a marker; he roughs it out with chisels and marks it with compasses.* —Isaiah 44:13

A skilled worker in wood would have understood all sorts of carpentry tasks. He would be able to make doors, window fittings, beds, chairs, footstools, bowls, and spoons. This same carpenter would make farming tools like ploughs, yokes, threshing instruments, and irrigation machines.

The wood available to a carpenter was the Lebanon cedar, cypress from Phoenicia, sycamore, olive, ebony, oak, ash, and boxwood. Cedar and cypress were imported and quite expensive.

Israeli carpenters were often considered second rate compared to the Phoenicians.

The metal workers usually had a good relationship with the carpenter since the wood and metal products often were used together, especially for farming tools. Copper was the most popular metal. When copper was mixed with tin, the strong alloy bronze was formed.

Objects that a metal worker would produce included needles, tweezers, pins, bracelets, bowls, pictures, urns, lamps, arrows, swords, and daggers.

Sample Carpenter Shop Script:
"All the best carpenters come from Bethlehem, you know. They are spread across Israel, but they all come from here. I saw a cousin of mine come through with his wife earlier. He lives in Nazareth now, but he's originally from here."

Sample Metal Shop Script:
"With my tools, you don't have to work so hard. They are solid and made very well. I tried to get a young man from Nazareth to buy my chisel, but he seemed too distracted by his wife's discomfort. Maybe I will see him when he leaves our town."

What to Do When Someone Visits Your Shop

- Allow visitors to test their skill with your tools. In the wood shop, guests can sand wood. In the metal shop, they can bang on the metal in an attempt to form it.
- Educate visitors on the tools and resources you use in your trades.

Apothecary Information

The apothecary was a combination of a pharmacist and a perfumer. The people there mixed and dispensed herbal medicines and also prepared perfumes and a wide range of cosmetics.

> *One of them went out into the fields to gather herbs and found a wild vine and picked as many of its gourds as his garment could hold.* —2 Kings 4:39

> *Woe to you Pharisees, because you give God a tenth of your mint, rue and all other kinds of garden herbs, but you neglect justice and the love of God.* —Luke 11:42

Common Remedies:

- If a patient complained of general ailments, including unexplained weight loss, the doctor would probably prescribe goat's milk. It was consumed frequently in the first century, and it was purported to be extremely healthy.
- Some physicians might recommend a mixture of barley porridge for physical difficulties.
- Good vegetables were also considered wholesome.
- In ancient days, mandrake leaves were often prescribed as a love potion.
- Honey was a widely-accepted tonic. Not only was it used for sore throats, but it also was applied directly to open wounds.
- Olive oil also helped heal ailments, whether ingested or rubbed on wounds.
- A stomach ache might bring remedies like rosemary, hyssop, rue, and certain kinds of palms. An irregular heartbeat could earn the patient a cup of barley soaked in curdled milk.
- Tarragon leaves were used to settle an upset stomach and stimulate a lost appetite. Brewed as a tea, it was reported to help sleep troubles. It was also chewed to numb a toothache.

Sample Apothecary Script:
"Ooh, that poor little mama, Mary, I gave her some mint tea to help her stomach ache, but I don't think a stomach ache was her problem. But welcome, come into my shop!"

What to Do When Someone Visits Your Shop

- Allow visitors to crush spices and smell them.
- Offer medical advice and apply some olive oil to help heal ailments.
- Offer mint tea as a way to treat stomach ache.

Weaver Information

God used weavers several times in Scripture to accomplish His purposes.

> *Every skilled woman spun with her hands and brought what she had spun—blue, purple, or scarlet yarn or fine linen.* —Exodus 35:25

> *He has filled them with skill to do all kinds of work as engravers, designers, embroiderers in blue, purple, and scarlet yarn and fine linen, and weavers—all of them skilled workers and designers.* —Exodus 35:35

Did you know the beam of the loom is mentioned in Judges 16:14 as the weapon Samson wielded against his ambushers?

To produce thread, the fibers (made from goat hair, sheep hair, or flax) had to be spun on a spindle. As the fibers are spun, they become smaller in diameter, but tight and stronger. A spinner would form a coarse thread with her fingers and fasten it to the spindle shaft. She loops this thread first around the lower end of the spindle and then around the upper end. Then she sets it spinning by twisting the spindle shaft between her fingers. She allows it to spin while feeding more fibers.

It would take more than 200 hours of spinning time to form enough thread to create a single garment! Add the gathering and weaving time, and it would take a total of 400 hours of work.

After the thread was spun, a weaver (usually a different person than the spinner) would use it in a loom to produce fabrics. Thread (called the warp) was attached to the beams of the loom, and a shuttle was used to weave cross-threads (called the weft) through them.

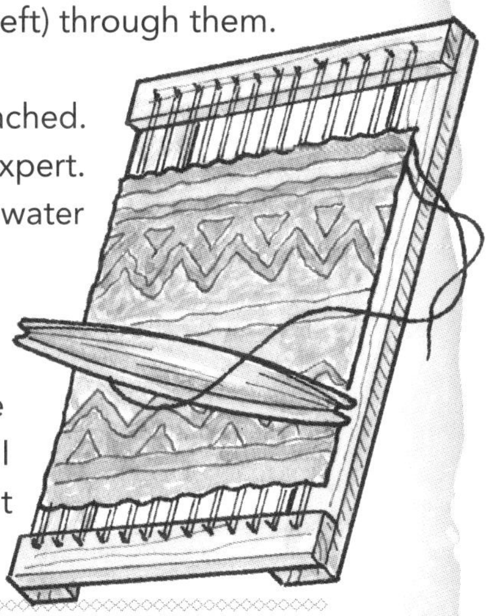

After the weaving process, the cloth needed to be washed or bleached. This process, called fulling, was usually performed by a separate expert. Fullers washed cloth by trampling it underfoot in shallow pools of water and then spreading it out to dry.

Sample Weaver Shop Script:
"I'm working on a blanket for someone right now. A young couple stopped in and asked for one. The husband is a distant cousin, so I am making this as a gift for their coming Baby. I just hope I can get it done before the Baby comes. That new mama looked so big!"

What to Do When Someone Visits Your Shop

- Invite visitors to practice their weaving on one of your small looms.
- Educate your guests on the details and skill that it took to make fabric.

Clothing Shop Information

Clothes have been popular ever since the days of Adam and Eve!

> *The LORD God made garments of skin for Adam and his wife and clothed them.* —Genesis 3:21

Making clothing in Bethlehem was a several-step process, and it took several people to accomplish the task:

1. Shepherds raised the sheep and sheared them every year.
2. Fullers were hired to wash the wool.
3. Spinners would take the raw wool and spin it into thread.
4. Dyers would dip the skeins of thread into steaming vats to give it the desired color.
5. Weavers wove the thread together using their looms and created long sections of fabric.
6. Tailors cut, measured, and sewed the fabric to make garments.
7. Embroiderers added style to the necklines by using decorative threads..
8. Jewelers might create ornamental clasps or pins for the belt, waist, or shoulders.

All told, it could take as much as 400 hours to create one garment!

The most common garment was a tunic. A tunic is essentially a large sack with holes cut in it for the head and arms. A cloth or leather belt (called a girdle) was used to hold it close to the body. Outside the tunic was a cloak. It was typically thicker and offered more protection. At night the owner would wrap himself in his cloak to sleep.

Sandals were the footwear of choice. They protected against the hot sand and were very cheap to buy. They were so common that only the poorest of the poor went without them.

The tunic, girdle, cloak, and sandals were worn by both men and women. By the time Jesus was born, women no longer wore a veil over their face at all times. Veils were used primarily as protection from sun and as a covering for prayer.

Sample Clothes Shop Script:
"I tried to sell some of these to that sweet…what was her name? Mary? Did you see her? Oh, I do hope they find a room. I was half afraid she would give birth right here in this shop!"

What to Do When Someone Visits Your Shop

- Allow visitors to try on some garments. Offer strips of fabric for visitors to keep as headbands.
- Teach your visitors about the common clothing of Bethlehem.

Jewelry Shop Information

Jewelry was a staple accessory during Bible times. Like many things, it could be used in a way that detracted from spiritual health, but other references reflect just the opposite as well: jewelry represented spiritual health and wealth.

> *All who were willing, men and women alike, came and brought gold jewelry of all kinds: brooches, earrings, rings and ornaments. They all presented their gold as a wave offering to the* *Lord.* —Exodus 35:22

> *We have brought as an offering to the Lord the gold articles each of us acquired—armlets, bracelets, signet rings, earrings and necklaces—to make atonement for ourselves before the Lord.* —Numbers 31:50

Bracelets and Anklets: The rich men wore bracelets or armlets. Most often, they were worn by nobility. The arm bands were formed from rare metals and encrusted with jewels. Anklets were worn by women as much for beauty as to make noise when the metal bands would clank together.

Chains: Government officials often had chains of gold placed on them as signs of their authority.

Signet ring: Worn on the finger or on a chain around the neck, this ring would have been used more for business than fashion. The markings on it were unique to the owner, and he would use it to seal documents and correspondence.

Sample Jewelry Shop Script:
"Many of my jewelry pieces are made from expensive gold and jewels. I take pride in what I do because it brings joy to my customers! Some people have never seen the likes of my jewelry. One young couple asked if I had any extra room in my home. Sadly, I did not, but I could tell they admired my work. I do hope they found a place to rest."

What to Do When Someone Visits Your Shop
- Let the visitors help you string beads to form a bracelet or necklace.
- Pass out bracelets to young guests.

Rope Maker Information

The Bible is full of references to people using ropes and cords. These important tools were used for:

- Raising or lowering weights (Joshua 2:15; Jeremiah 38:11)
- Harnessing or leading animals (Isaiah 5:18)
- Holding a tent (Isaiah 33:20)
- Hauling stones and throwing down fortifications (2 Samuel 17:13)
- Making snares or traps (Job 18:10)
- Tying prisoners (Judges 15:13; 16:11–12; Psalm 129:4; Ezekiel 3:25)
- Ships' tackle (Isaiah 33:23)
- Measuring tools (2 Samuel 8:2)

The Hebrew word for rope is "Hebel." The Hebrew word for cord is "Abot."

Rope makers typically used animal hair or strips of skin to make their ropes.

Rope was inexpensive and only the poor people would be caught wearing it as a garment.

A wide variety of knots were tied and used, depending on their different purposes and amount of weight the knots would hold.

Figure 8 Knot

Reef Knot

Sheep Shank Knot

Sample Rope Maker Script:
"I started out as an apprentice rope maker before joining the family business. Now I can tie knots faster than anyone! I think I impressed the young carpenter with my skills, but his wife was too uncomfortable to care."

What to Do When Someone Visits Your Shop

- Hand out pieces of twine as free samples of your handiwork.
- Teach them to tie various knots with the twine.
- Unbraid some of the ropes in your shop and allow guests to braid them back together.

Scribe Information

Many Bible verses support the employment and respect of a scribe as well as the act of writing.

> *Jonathan, David's uncle, was a counselor, a man of insight and a scribe.*
> —1 Chronicles 27:32

> *Jeremiah took another scroll and gave it to the scribe Baruch son of Neriah, and as Jeremiah dictated, Baruch wrote on it all the words of the scroll.* —Jeremiah 36:32

> *Write this down, for these words are trustworthy and true.* —Revelation 21:5

The scribe profession is very old and highly regarded. Records indicate scribes were employed as early as 3,000 B.C. Their tasks varied, from public secretary who transcribed legal contracts, to letter writer or accountant. A scribe typically did all this from dictation.

A scribe was responsible for preserving Scripture by copying it. He also was an expert in the Hebrew language, and were it not for his work, the Hebrew language might have died out.

A scribe was meticulous in his work. Because printing presses and copy machines didn't exist, exactness in spelling, crowning certain letters, dotting others, and following prescribed regulations as to spacing for sections was mandatory.

Since scribes became so familiar with the text of Scripture, they often were looked to for direction in interpreting difficult passages. Along with rabbis, scribes were the spiritual leaders.

Scribes were also known as counters. This name developed because a good scribe knew how many letters were in each book of the Bible. After copying a book, he would go back through and count to make sure he got them all.

Here are some samples. Remember Hebrew is writen from right to left.

הבהא	םיהולא	קוֹנִית	םוֹלָשׁ	ןֵב	תַב
love	God	baby	peace	son	daughter

Sample Scribe Script:
"What do you want me to write…your name? I can write your name, just like I wrote the name of that young man and his wife from…where were they from? Oh, yes, Nazareth! Such a long way off! And they looked tired, but I digress. Let me write your name!"

What to Do When Someone Visits Your Shop

- Inform visitors about the details of your job and ask if there's anything they need recorded or copied. Provide paint and parchment and help visitors create Hebrew words with the paint provided.

Games Information

Although the life of a Jewish person in the ancient world was a hard one, it wasn't all work and no play.

> *God was with the boy as he grew up. He lived in the desert and became an archer.*
> —Genesis 21:20

> *The city streets will be filled with boys and girls playing.* —Zechariah 8:5

Very little has changed over the centuries when it comes to children's toys. Small children played with rattles and whistles. Little girls had dollhouses, complete with little pottery furnishings. Some dolls had jointed arms and legs, with beads for hair. They also used puppets on strings and pull toys on wheels (similar to wagons). One of the most common toys was a simple leather ball to play catch with.

Though games like Monopoly, Scrabble, and Uno were not yet played, the families did have many games. Hopscotch, marbles, and leather balls were used all the time. The leather balls were used to toss back and forth as well as to juggle.

Board games were widely played as well. Many of our strategy games such as chess and checkers have their foundations in ancient times. They would use pieces to move along the board and would roll dice. Dice games were taken very seriously. One game played frequently was similar to the current game of "Life." Instead of going to school, getting a job, marrying, and filling the car with kids, players moved their pieces around to be robed, crowned, and sceptered. Then the first player to complete the game was declared king and would win all of the money put down on the game.

In ancient times, there were three forms of dice used in games. One was a flat coin, with one side painted black and the other white. These types of dice were used in divining the will of God, as with the Urim and Thummim (Exodus 28:30). When these lots were cast, two white lots meant "yes," two black lots meant "no," and a combination meant to wait. The second type of dice was a four-sided die shaped like a pyramid. The last die was a basic cube. These six-sided dice were very popular, especially with the Romans, and were probably what was used at the foot of the cross when Jesus was dying (see Matthew 27:35).

Both adults and children enjoyed using weapons for target practice. The most common were bow and arrows and slingshots. Slingshots used two strings connected to one pouch and would be spun rapidly over a person's head. The person would then let go of one string at the right time and throw the stones in whatever direction they wanted. This was a simple slingshot, much like what David used to defeat Goliath (see 1 Samuel 17:50).

Top 10 Ancient Family Games

- Marbles
- Hopscotch
- Juggling
- Archery
- Wrestling
- Bowling
- Catch
- Slingshot Practice
- Foot Races
- Mancala

Sample Games Script:
"Come try one of my games! I bet you are very good. Can you juggle? Sling the rock at that object? Keep the marbles in the circle? I will show you the secrets to doing well at these games!"

What to Do When Someone Visits Your Shop

- Educate them on the games that were played in Bethlehem.
- Invite them to play some games with you and your family.

Final Layer

The Soldiers

The villagers' lives are frequently interrupted by the intimidating rulers of the time, namely soldiers and mercenaries. These individuals served the Roman establishment above all else, so their treatment of anyone who presented even the smallest of loyalties to another king (god) was severely mistreated. Most of the Jewish people were taxed to the point of near impoverishment.

If you have the volunteer capacity, consider casting one, two, or three soldiers who walk around looking "tough." They don't have to say much, as their mere presence inspires looks of fear and silent disdain from the villagers.

Unexpected "Actors"

Many outreaches offer an animal area where churches bring in donkeys, sheep, cattle, and even camels. While this added touch requires some extra thought and expense, the outcome is very positive. Almost every church mentioned the use of animals in their town.

Mary Ann Randolph, pastor of church life and discipleship at East Side Church of God in Anderson, Indiana, said animals have always been a big hit at their outreach. In 2018, they had a camel. "Tons of kids were just fascinated with the camel. They just kept coming back to see it."

A lady who attended the Live Nativity at our church stopped in and gave a donation. She said she wanted to do something because we are "a light" in our community.... Many people refer to us as "the nativity church."

—Mark Ferren, Children's Pastor, Searcy First Assembly Church, Searcy, AR

Chapter 8

Creating Costumes: The Attire

We are in our second year of putting on our [Christmas outreach], so we're still learning and growing. Our costumes are a combination of borrowing and getting our own. We borrowed some costumes from another church; we're grateful they were willing to share. We're also making costumes; they're just simple and basic robes. We gather sheets from Goodwill to make them from. Seamstresses from inside our church sew them together or make head scarves for us.

—Kimberly Tussing, Children's Ministry Director, Mountain Park Church, Phoenix, AZ

Clothing worn by the Hebrew people reflected their values and spiritual beliefs:

> *I delight greatly in the Lord; my soul rejoices in my God. For he has clothed me with garments of salvation and arrayed me in a robe of his righteousness, as a bridegroom adorns his head like a priest, and as a bride adorns herself with her jewels.* —Isaiah 61:10

Clothing worn by the Hebrew people during Bible times was graceful, modest, and exceedingly significant. Often a man's clothing indicated his profession, such as the rabbi's blue-fringed robe. Their clothing also was an external symbol of internal feelings. When joyful and ready to enter into festive occasions, they wore clothing of vivid colors. When they humbled themselves or were in mourning, they wore sackcloth.

In everyday life, men and women alike wore two-layered tunics, or simple one-piece robes, belted at the waist with two holes for the arms. The first layer fit more like a long T-shirt, and the second, or outer tunic, was longer and more flowing.

For women, their outer tunics were longer, covering their legs and even their feet. Women oftentimes wore aprons over their tunics to protect their clothing and also help them carry things. Many times, women's garments were embellished with needlework, embossing, and embroidery.

In cooler weather, the Israelites might wear a cloak over the tunics to help keep them warm.

Headwear: Men wore a folded square piece of cloth as a veil for protection from the sun or wrapped it around as a turban. Later on, pieces of cloth were twisted around the head. There is some debate as to whether women wore a face veil all the time, or if they wore them primarily in the temple or synagogue.

Imagine the head covering as a piece of cloth that extended to and around the shoulders, then tied at the forehead.

Footwear: The poor people often went barefoot. Others wore sandals. Sandals had soles made of wood, cane, or palm tree bark fastened to the leather by nails and tied to the feet and legs with leather. Slippers of soft leather were also worn by wealthier people.

Jewelry: Men and women wore earrings, signet rings (worn around the neck on a cord), and chains. Women commonly wore nose rings, bracelets, and anklets.

Roman Soldiers

Roman soldiers were clothed in red tunics with varying lengths, according to the rank of the wearer. Roman soldiers serving in cooler climates also wore trousers of varying lengths, from just above the knee or to the ankles, and fastened at the waist with a drawstring. Cloaks were similar to capes or ponchos we wear today.

They also wore military belts as well as leg wrappings made from strips of material or leather, extending from the ankle up to right above the calf. They wore military sandals or boots. Finally, the soldiers wore a type of apron, made of leather, that was more for making noise and intimidating viewers than for any kind of protection.

Soldiers' protective garments, usually made of metal, included helmets, as well as shoulder, arm, and leg guards. They wore breastplates, and they carried shields and swords.

Acquiring the Costumes

Costumes can be acquired by any number of means. They can be purchased online, with prices determined by the level of quality of the costumes. For example, Oriental Trading sells costumes beginning at $15.00, but the quality is such that the costumes might last for only one or two seasons. Other online costume companies offer not only costumes, but also wigs, sandals, headpieces, and other props related to costumes.

Another way to acquire costumes is to make them. Purchase several bolts of muslin fabric as well as lightweight fabric of different colors. The muslin fabric can be cut in the shape of a tunic with the sides glued together using fabric glue. If a seamstress is available, instead of gluing the fabric, the sides can be sewn together. Many tutorials exist online for using this process.

You also can purchase sheets and towels from your local thrift store to make costumes.

Warner Press offers a tutorial on designing your own costumes. You can view the tutorial online at: WarnerPress.org/RecreatingChristmas-freeresources.

If you want something a bit more sophisticated and you have a seamstress, pattern companies make patterns for costumes. These patterns also recommend specific types of fabrics. Visit a fabric store to see these patterns.

A third way of acquiring costumes is to rent them from costume rental companies or local schools. These tend to be a higher quality, but the negative side is your church doesn't own the costumes after the event.

A final way is to borrow the costumes. If another church has performed a similar event in the past or even held a Vacation Bible School with a similar theme, they just may have costumes on hand that they would be more than happy to share.

To churches who are just starting, I would encourage you to start somewhere. When I was a teenager, my brother and I made a stick hut at the corner of the church parking lot. We dressed up like shepherds, and we had sheep and a donkey. We did that three or four years with our youth pastor. Now, I'm 50.... It's so different now. Our [outreach] is massive.

—Mark Ferren, Children's Pastor, Searcy First Assembly Church, Searcy, AR

Chapter 9

Building the Town: The Scenes

We use both wood and Styrofoam to build our props. Styrofoam makes the props look realistic. We order our Styrofoam from a local plant. We use a two-pound density, but churches can also use a one-pound density that's less expensive. We had a two-inch thick Styrofoam front gate that lasted for 12 years.... We order palm trees from a nursery in Ozark, Missouri.

—Mark Ferren, Children's Pastor, Searcy First Assembly Church, Searcy, AR

Imagine the sights and sounds of Bethlehem in AD 1. The fragrance of baking bread and sweet olive oil waft through the arid breeze. The clanging of hammers against nails echoes along the streets as carpenters shape their wood. One shopkeeper greets another as lambs escape their fenced area, baaing through the gate. Re-creating Christmas starts to significantly take shape with the scenery. While all the pieces are important in the creation of a live Christmas story, the building of the town makes the effort seem real.

> *My people will live in peaceful dwelling places, in secure homes, in undisturbed places of rest.* —Isaiah 32:18

> *They will build houses and dwell in them; they will plant vineyards and eat their fruit. No longer will they build houses and others live in them, or plant and others eat. For as the days of a tree, so will be the days of my people; my chosen ones will long enjoy the work of their hands.* —Isaiah 65:21–22

Similar to our homes today that are constructed with different materials, homes in AD 1 also were built with different materials, based on accessibility and wealth.

Tents were most commonly used early in the Old Testament because of the Israelites' nomadic way of life. Families had to move their sheep where grass and water were readily available.

While tents also were dwelling places in the New Testament (although not as much as in the Old Testament), homes also were made in caves along the hillsides in Bethlehem.

Stones and bricks were also available. Stones were part of the terrain, and bricks were made by mixing mud and straw together. Mortar, also made from natural materials, was used to hold the pieces together.

While these different types of homes existed throughout Palestine, the homes in your event are made much more simply. Given today's readily-available information on "DIY" websites and Pinterest, you have access to many tutorials on how to create your town. To make your search simpler, Warner Press offers free video tutorials online at WarnerPress.org/RecreatingChristmas-freeresources.

The remainder of this chapter provides four different ways to build your village: using canopies and tents, using foamboard, using fabric sheets, and making wooden sheds.

Use Tents and Canopies
This style is especially nice if you have a large, single room to gather in such as a multipurpose room or a gymnasium.

Use the frames from pop-up tents or pop-up canopies. Then, layer large pieces of fabric over the frames, draping the fabric to create interesting levels and textures for your home. Or you could spread hay over the tops to represent a sort of thatched roof. Pin back the front sides so your guests feel welcome to come into your home/shop. Add a table and some pillows to your "home," and decorate according to the theme of your shop.

Set the homes up side-by-side around the perimeter of the room, and Bethlehem's town guests can venture in and out of the shops.

Use Foamboard

Foamboard is great to use when you want to transform smaller rooms or Sunday school classrooms into your Bethlehem village. The biggest transformation takes place when you make walls that look like stone homes and storefronts; however, if you desire a more authentic, textured look, creating stone walls takes time, usually about one hour per wall. Plus, making the foam walls is a messy process. Nevertheless, the effort pays off when you make a fairly authentic-looking wall for your Bethlehem home.

Be sure to purchase ¾″ foam boards from a local big box home store such as Home Depot, Menard's, or Lowe's. Ask for the 4′x8′ size. These boards cost in the vicinity of $20.00 per sheet, so each room may cost upward of $120.00 for the foam boards.

Before designing, be sure to remove the plastic sheeting.

Draw the outlines of your stones with a marker. Then, using a home power drill with a ¾″ diameter wire brush attachment, lightly brush over the outlines of the stones to create a variegated look.

Then purchase two cans of inexpensive latex paint, one in dark brown and another in white, to create three different shades.

Purchase three paint trays for mixing paint, paint stirrers, rollers, and brushes, and several sea sponges.

Mix together brown and white paints to create the lightest shade of brown for the base coat. Paint entire board with this color. Use brushes to paint the crevices of the mortar.

Then mix the medium shade of brown by using equal parts of dark brown and white. This color will be used for the face of the stones. Dab on the paint using the sea sponge, allowing the base coat to show through for texture. Avoid getting this darker shade onto the mortar area.

Mix the darkest shade of brown, using more dark brown paint than white. You will use the least amount of this shade. Dab this darkest shade onto some of the faces of the stones for texture.

Go back to the medium brown paint to add more texture yet. The darkest shade doesn't have to be completely dry. If you prefer, you can dab on the lightest for even more texture.

This process makes for a very nice stone façade.

Use Fabric, Drop Cloth Canvas, or Bulletin Board Paper
This method is probably the least expensive method and is ideal for smaller budgets and can be used in smaller rooms such as Sunday school rooms. The down side to working with these types of material is that it is more difficult to achieve a realistic look.

You basically use the same painting method as above, but add a fourth, lighter color to paint the mortar instead of using a drill with a brush attachment.

To hang the faux wall, first place painter's tape on the wall. Then neatly cover the tape with hot glue and lay the fabric or paper onto the glue.

Use Wood
Wood might be a reasonable way to go financially, especially if your church has access to scrap wood or pallets. (Many businesses are looking for people to take pallets off their hands.) Plus, wooden shops/homes are much more durable. The problem arises in where to store the small sheds year after year.

Wooden shops also might not be quite as time-consuming as painting and hanging paper, fabric, or foam board, but this method certainly requires someone who knows how to measure, cut with a saw, and hammer the wood together.

The sheds don't have to be perfect; it only adds to the authenticity if slight gaps appear here and there.

Whether you purchase wood, find scrap wood, use particle board, or even repurpose pallet wood, once again, several tutorials exist online, along with free tutorials at WarnerPress.org/RecreatingChristmas-freeresources. Better still, find a local friendly carpenter who can draw a simple plan.

Final Touches

Finally, decorate the home and shop thematically, according to the type of shop each family will "own." Add straw, pillows, a small table, and props such as pottery, jewelry pieces, or food.

Recall the primary characters from chapter 5 who are necessary to tell the Christmas story accurately; be sure these characters have their own shelter, whether that place is a shed, a tent, or a stone home. Then, fill in other areas with the villagers' store fronts.

Some shops might be better off just to place their wares on rustic tables or even inside old wooden wheelbarrows or carts. Shorter tables, wooden benches, or hay bales might be appropriate for sitting around for crafts or eating snacks.

Creating realistic scenes immerses your guests, most of them unchurched, into the life-changing reality of Christ. This personal engagement allows them to experience the truth that Jesus came for each one of them. It will be so worth the effort to watch the Kingdom grow to the point where someday in Heaven, an individual will say, "My life changed because I came to a Christmas event at your church."

> *I bring you good news that will cause great joy for all the people. Today in the town of David a Savior has been born to you; he is the Messiah, the Lord.*— Luke 2:10–11

We had talked about doing our [outreach] one more year and then assessing whether or not we would continue. We held it earlier in December than we normally would. Afterwards one of our volunteers was in line at Walmart and struck up a conversation with a stranger. This person was going through a very difficult time of life. At the last minute, her son and she went to the nativity, and when they got home, her son said to her, "I have to tell you something. Before we went tonight, I had decided I was going to kill myself. But after tonight, I feel like I really have hope."

That was a transformative moment for our church, and we decided to continue. If in our 40 years of presenting [our outreach] we helped save a life by offering the hope of Christ, that's enough of a reason for me to continue doing it.

—Steve DeLisle, Pastor, Maple Grove Church of God, Anderson, IN

Chapter 10

Practicing Hospitality: The Touch Points

One of the things we did differently this year was eliminate having guests register so the evening was more about having fun. We also had tour guides take guests through the town instead of being told the story and having them explore on their own. The guides told the story as they led the tour and helped make the connection between the actors and the guests. It made things more personal and helped everyone relax a bit.

—Mary Ann Randolph, Pastor of Church Life and Discipleship, Eastside Church of God, Anderson, IN

Whether or not they have chosen to be transformed by its power, the Christmas narrative isn't new for most American people. Our job in Re-creating Christmas is to help them experience the story in a different way, a way that moves them from knowing about the story to knowing the story personally, in a way that will transform their hearts.

We have the privilege of being change agents, and one of the best ways to initiate change is by showing hospitality. For this event, we show love through welcoming our guests and helping them to feel at ease.

> *Love each other deeply, because love covers over a multitude of sins. Offer hospitality to one another without grumbling.* —1 Peter 4:8–9

> *Do not forget to show hospitality to strangers, for by so doing some people have shown hospitality to angels without knowing it.* —Hebrews 13:2

> *Love your neighbor as yourself.* —Matthew 22:39

Generally speaking, our culture has lost its welcoming spirit. In the spirit of "freedom," we say what we want to say however we want to say it, we express more impatience and less compassion, more hostility and less empathy in our interactions. We have reduced conversations to text messages made of two or three words and an emoji instead of looking someone in the eye and asking them about their day.

Christians have such a great opportunity to be different from the world in this area simply by being kind and warmly welcoming those who attend our outreach. We can safely assume many who come to the outreach are tired from striving or maybe haven't heard a kind word from another person in a while. A joyful "hello" or brief interaction with a guest has the powerful potential for that guest to think, "This is a friendly place. I felt welcome. I think I'll come back."

A person doesn't have to have the spiritual gift of hospitality to have a spirit of hospitality. At its essence, hospitality is one person communicating to another person, whether in word, body language, or facial expression the message, "Because you are made in the image of God and are His child, I value you." Hospitality is a smile given, eye contact made, words of welcome expressed. Hospitality toward an unbeliever is even more important because we are expressing the heart of Christ to those who do not know Him.

General Welcome Statements

Briefly instruct your villagers to welcome others with the following words:

"Thank you for coming to visit our village!"

"We have been expecting you and are glad you are here!"

"Are you hungry? We have many snacks from our area of the world to share with you."

"Would you like to learn about a new game?"

"How far did you travel? Where are you from? How far is that from Bethlehem?"

"Can I help you with…(your coats? your umbrellas? your diaper bag?)"

"Can I show you where you need to go?"

Specific Touch Points

Not only should your volunteers welcome your guests in general ways, your church should consider specific touch points, or high impact moments, for showing hospitality to the public.

The first touch point is in parking. Direct people in their parking efforts, particularly if your event has attracted a large following. No matter the age, parking attendants can smile as they wave their visitors into the parking area. Volunteers can also be aware of special needs, such as helping the elderly or a single parent. If possible, offer valet parking to those visitors. Some churches might even have a golf cart where they can drive visitors from the parking area to the outreach area.

A second touch point is the front door. People with a friendly countenance should open the front door, as this is a first impression as to how welcoming the church is. If a greeter is shy or has a hard time looking a guest in the eye, it might be better to find a different greeter. Ideally, these greeters should be dressed in costume in order to immerse guests in the Bethlehem experience.

A third touch point is the entrance into the town of Bethlehem as this is a transitional point in their experience. Situate greeters here, dressed in first century attire, who can say, "Welcome to Bethlehem! We have many guests who are here to be counted for the census. Don't worry though; we won't make you pay taxes. On the contrary, we would like to invite you to visit our village marketplace! The Roman soldiers ordinarily are grumpy, but today, they're all in a pretty good mood!"

Of course, villagers with their storefronts add to the warmth of the town when these first century citizens also greet their new visitors. As they lightheartedly banter back and forth with each other as well as introduce themselves to the newcomers, inviting them to their shop or to try a new food, they're practicing hospitality.

A more obvious touch point is with the kids. More than likely, families are attending this event because they want to create happy holiday memories with their children. A parent's joy oftentimes is connected to a child's joy, so if children have a great experience, so will their parents.

Place extra effort on creating special moments with the children. Shake their hands; offer craft opportunities and fun food. Create a celebratory spirit, and kids will never forget this time. If this event is important to the youngsters, it becomes equally important to the grown-ups who attend with them.

A final and important touch point occurs when visitors are leaving your property. Your church definitely wants to invite guests to the upcoming service(s) where the message will focus on the meaning of the first Christmas. This moment should be bestowed with sincere grace and warmth, as it is the last impression of the evening.

Be prepared to offer an invitation with your church service times. A verbal invitation, postcard, a treat with service information, or something else they can keep as a reminder are all ideal forms of invitations. The next chapter offers more detail on this topic.

College students volunteered in the craft room. While families made the crafts, our staff and other volunteers could interact with the visitors. Later, as people were leaving, they would comment, "We couldn't get our kids to leave the craft room!" Having that time for kids and parents to sit and create something together was special for everyone.

—Mary Ann Randolph, Pastor of Church Life and Discipleship,
Eastside Church of God, Anderson, IN

We have very good greeters who are welcoming. We have a refreshment time where we offer cookies, hot chocolate, and coffee. We spread out scrapbooks with pictures of all the years we've offered our [event]. People in our church introduce themselves and tell stories. This is a very meaningful time for visitors.

—Steve DeLisle, Pastor, Maple Grove Church of God, Anderson, IN

Chapter 11

Spreading the Word: The Invitation

I encourage our church to take plates of cookies to their neighbors, offer them some baked goods, and invite them. This creates a connection, a relationship. We have found people are more willing to come to church at Christmas, so they're more open.
—Steve DeLisle, Pastor, Maple Grove Church of God, Anderson, IN

We all have had those awkward experiences when either we didn't know whether or not we were invited to an event, or we simply assumed we were uninvited when we wanted to be invited. Maybe the word didn't get to us individually, or the invitation arrived late. Whatever the circumstances, we just knew we wanted to be part of the celebration and felt overlooked when we weren't included.

You can more than avoid these types of awkward moments in Re-creating Christmas by making sure everyone is invited to the big event. All you need is a plan and a little bit of know-how. Fortunately, both are covered in this chapter.

> *This gospel of the kingdom will be proclaimed throughout the whole world as a testimony to all nations.* —Matthew 24:14 (ESV)

> *Let us go…and see this thing that has happened, which the Lord has made known to us.*
> — Luke 2:15 (ESV)

The Plan

The best invitation comes in many forms, from a physical invitation, to a website, or even social media. However, nothing trumps the personal invitation.

Early on in the process, begin asking the congregation to pray and think about the people they would like to invite. Then, encourage them to think about ways they can extend an invitation in a natural way. For example, if a church member is spending some scheduled time outside of work and church to help prepare for the outreach, he or she might want to share that project with a neighbor, which of course, leads to natural conversation about the event.

Another important component to the invitation process is to create physical invitations. Have quality postcard-size and business card-size invitations printed and available for churchgoers to freely pick up as they come in and out of the church building. Even if your church is on a budget, you want the invitations to look excellent, as they reflect the level of excellence of your event. So, spend some money to distribute professionally-designed promotional materials. Maybe someone in your church is a graphic designer who is willing to donate time and energy to designing the materials. Maybe a local designer is willing to give a discount for your project. No matter how you go about printing the supplies, it's important to give something to the church members and their kids to share with others. Some towns have schools that are willing to place an invitation in their school newsletter. It never hurts to ask!

Printed posters are also a great idea. Many towns have libraries, grocery stores, banks, and other public places with bulletin boards where these posters can be attached.

Purchase ad space in your local newspaper, if your town still relies on getting their community news in this format.

You can find ready-made art for invitations, posters, and a newspaper ad, online at WarnerPress.org/RecreatingChristmas-freeresources. These supplemental materials are created in such a way that you can download onto your computer, add your information, and then print off either at your church or your local printer. These ready-made materials offer the words, "Make New Memories with Christmas Comes to Town," providing the name "Christmas Comes to Town" for your event.

Another idea is to participate in a fall craft show and sell or hand out something special the Bethlehem marketplace might be sharing the evening of your event; then, extend an invitation in that context.

Of course, what you say on the invitation is as important as the invitation itself. Obviously, you want to provide the date, time, location, and the fact that the event is free. If school-age children are involved, encourage the community to support their youth.

You also want to come up with a creative, compelling slogan for your invitation. For example, you might say, "Make New Memories" or "Tired of the Same Christmas Traditions?" Speaking directly to families and providing them with opportunities to experience something new is an attractive enticement most people don't want to pass up, especially when it involves the entire family and the event is free.

This event is the perfect time to use technology for Kingdom purposes. Create a Facebook page separate from your church Facebook page. Name the page the same as the name of the event. Then, on the Facebook page, create an event. Do the same with Instagram, Twitter, and other social media platforms. Request family members to use the same hashtags the church provides. Encourage families also to take funny Christmas photos to post online about the event.

Some churches might want even to take that extra step and create a separate website for the outreach. Several hosting sites have free website templates. All your volunteer has to do is drag and drop text or images. Today's domains cost only about $35.00 for an entire year and are renewable for subsequent years' use. Give the domain the same name as the event and include the town's name in the domain. For example, you might name it: ChristmasComestoCincinnati.com. or Cincinnati.ChristmasComestoTown.com. Incorporating your town's name often helps in search engine optimization. When someone googles "Christmas events near me," hopefully your church's event will pop up on the first one or two pages of the search.

The Know-How

Your church doesn't have to create these promotional materials on their own. The more volunteers or even community individuals you can get involved, the more people there are to take ownership in the Christmas outreach. Call on those church members who have the design capabilities or technological aptitude to help. Solicit a local college or high school class to design the materials. Ask local businesses for a discount on their services; some places are willing to help their community churches that have limited resources.

Be clear in your wishes and provide public positive accolades to all who help.

Most of all, ask God to give your church the vision; ask Him to bring people and opportunities your way to accomplish the tasks. He will, because He is good and delights to bless His children.

Post-Event Invitations

After you host your Christmas outreach, be sure to invite guests to return for your Christmas Sunday celebration. An ideal situation would be to appoint a pastor as a final touchpoint at your outreach event and then have him or her initiate the invitation, both through word and through a physical card. Doing so communicates to the family that they are valued and welcomed into our church body.

Another way to reach out might be to have an email sheet where guests provide the church with their email addresses. After the Christmas outreach, the pastor can send an email to those visitors and invite them to the church Christmas service.

A final way to reach out is once again capitalize on technology. Create follow-up messages on social media thanking guests for visiting the event and invite them to return on Christmas Sunday.

Regardless of the methods your church chooses to use to get the word out, the ultimate goal is to extend a sense of belonging. When individuals communicate to their neighbors and guests, "I value you. I value your family," that authentic message makes it hard for people to say no.

Be filled with love that comes from a pure heart, a clear conscience, and genuine faith.
— 1 Timothy 1:5 (NLT)

We build a float for our local Christmas parade where we have a nativity scene and we invite people to [our event]. Doing this tells a story for not a lot of money, plus we're one of the very few floats with a Christian message.
—Steve DeLisle, Pastor, Maple Grove Church of God, Anderson, IN

We started our event ten years ago. The first year, my husband and I were on the way to church, and I asked him, "Do you think anybody will come?" We had about 1,600 people attend that first year. Last year we had over 3,500 people. Imagine that many people hearing the Good News that Jesus came for them!
—Fran Emmons, GraceWay Bible Church, Hamilton, NJ

Chapter 12

Reaching Out: The Follow Up

It's fun to meet new people. Many of my "animal people" [people who bring in live animals] either go to other churches or don't go to church at all. It's a lot of work for the sheep farmers to get their sheep here without losing any. When one jumps out, the others do, too! What are you going to do with a loose sheep in Gig Harbor!

—Gayle Shriner, Discovery Baptist, Gig Harbor, WA

Hospitality begins at the entrance of Re-creating Christmas and extends until guests get into their cars to leave the outreach. Nothing communicates care and acceptance more than a sincere smile and gracious gesture.

Since the primary reason for your outreach is to expose the community to God's generosity in sending Jesus into the world, one of the most important components to your outreach event is creating a follow-up plan. This moment just might be the most important part of the experience. These last few minutes with a family might determine whether or not they will feel comfortable walking through your church doors on the following Sunday.

> *I was hungry and you gave me something to eat, I was thirsty and you gave me something to drink, I was a stranger and you invited me in, I needed clothes and you clothed me, I was sick and you looked after me, I was in prison and you came to visit me.... Truly I tell you, whatever you did for one of the least of these brothers and sisters of mine, you did for me.*
> — Matthew 25:35–36, 40

When individuals don't "look" or behave the same as our Christian friends, sometimes it's easy to forget they deserve the same kindness we would offer Christ. Thinking about and planning for these important interactions is critical not just for the success of your event, but more importantly, for the Kingdom.

If at all possible, have your pastor and spouse situated toward the exit; they are the primary faces of your church on a Sunday when the lead pastor stands in front of the congregation to speak. If they are unavailable, situate someone from your church who is very outgoing, helpful, and unafraid to engage guests in conversations.

These individuals can ask families how they enjoyed their experience, what they learned, and engage children by asking what their favorite part of the experience was.

Ask for Contact Information

Of course, a follow up should also have a component where your church can receive guests' contact information. Most people won't stand and fill out a contact form, but they might provide their information if some sort of incentive is offered.

One creative way to receive contact information is to create a photo booth at your event. Decorate the area with stars or a manger scene. Or, you can go in the opposite direction and offer a winter scene with a Candy Land theme. Offer guests an opportunity to have their pictures taken for free. They will need to provide you with an email for you to send a digital image of their family picture. Or, they can "like" and "follow" your Christmas outreach name on Facebook, and you can provide a link to a family's image from there.

Other ideas to consider when trying to get contact information include:

- Offer a sign up for a drawing for a free meal and Christmas caroling.
- Ask a local coffee shop or restaurant to provide a coupon for a free drink or discount. If guests provide contact information, they receive the coupon. This invitation can be extended digitally, as well, when guests visit a website or Facebook page. The coupon could be downloaded once they type in their information.
- A donation is given to a local charity or food pantry when information is provided.
- Your church might also offer family-friendly Christmas stories or devotionals online when guests fill out a form.

Explain to your guests that your church won't annoy them with constant emails or phone calls, but you might send a thank you note and invitation to church.

Whatever form your church takes in receiving guest information, visitors definitely should receive an invitation to church the following Sunday, where Christmas carols will be sung, and the Christmas story will be told. Invite them both verbally and send them away with a postcard invitation.

Provide a Take-Home Packet

Another way to extend hospitality while also receiving contact information is to provide take-home packets for visitors. These packets can contain all the information listed above, along with any of the following:

- Activity pages for kids
- Paper nativity cut-outs for families to set up in their homes
- An opportunity to participate in a survey that provides feedback about the event. After the survey is completed (online),

families receive a downloadable gift such as music, gift certificate, or delivered home-made cookies.

- Kid-friendly book or booklet about the Christmas story
- Christmas ornament activity
- Packages of hot chocolate

Make sure the packet also includes an invitation to return to church on the following Sunday.

You can find activity sheets to download and print off as well as recipes online at WarnerPress.org/RecreatingChristmas-freeresources.

Researchers suggest having guests complete any online information within 36 hours of the event while the experience still has significance and impact on the family; otherwise, receiving information is substantially diminished.

Offer Hope

Some people are unconnected to a church because they have been hurt by someone in the church. Others are unconnected because they feel unworthy. Still others are unconnected because they feel little hope in their circumstances. Maybe they don't see a need for the church. With Re-creating Christmas, we can begin to change the narrative they live. We can be the hope Jesus offers. We can take steps to help them trust the church again. We can help them feel loved and accepted.

When we reach out to others, we help them reach up to God.

> *This year, our city's mall closed down, which was where many children would go to visit Santa, so we decided to bring Santa to our event. This was new to our church and it ended up working out great. A photographer took pictures of kids with Santa, and we collected families' contact information for them to get the pictures. We heard a lot of positive comments.*
>
> —Mary Ann Randolph, Pastor of Church Life and Discipleship,
> Eastside Church of God, Anderson, IN

Appendix

With the purchase of this book, you have access to many free, downloadable items to help equip your church for your outreach.

Log onto: WarnerPress.org/RecreatingChristmas-freeresources.

You will be directed to a site that contains the following:

- A promotional video to recruit volunteers and inform your church about the event
- Helpful DIY videos for building your town, making props, and fashioning costumes
- Recipes
- Postcard, newspaper ad, and sign templates
- Kids coloring and activity pages

Check back often on this page as we continue to add more resources!

Notes:

Notes: